VOICES OF COLOR

EDITED AND WITH AN INTRODUCTION BY
YOLANDA ALANIZ &
NELLIE WONG

Red Letter Press ∽ Seattle

© 1999 by Red Letter Press
409 Maynard Avenue South, Suite 201
Seattle, WA 98104 • (206) 682-0990
RedLetterPress@juno.com
Printed in the United States of America

First Edition. 1999

Library of Congress Cataloging-in-Publication Data
Voices of color /
edited and with an introduction by
Yolanda Alaniz & Nellie Wong.—1st ed.
p.   cm.
Includes index.
ISBN 0-932323-05-7 (pbk.)
1. Minorities—United States—Social conditions.
2. Minorities—United States—Political activity.
3. Minority women—United States.
4. Feminism—United States.
I. Alaniz, Yolanda, 1950-   .   II. Wong, Nellie.
E184.A1V7   1998
305.8'00973—DC21   98-21193

Book design: Susan McDonald
Cover design: Helen Gilbert
Cover photo: University of California students demonstrate in
defense of affirmative action on July 20, 1995 in San Francisco.
Photo by Rick Gerharter © 1995, Impact Visuals.

Articles reprinted by permission of the *Freedom Socialist*
newspaper, which commissioned their writing.
"You were born" ©1995 by Nellie Wong,
reprinted by permission of the author.

Sources of border designs:
Ziva Amir, *Arabesque: Decorative Needlework from the Holy Land.*
W. & G. Audsley, *Designs and Patterns from Historic Ornament.*
Jorge Enciso, *Design Motifs of Ancient Mexico.*
Frances Paul, *Spruce Root Basketry of the Alaska Tlinget.*
Geoffrey Williams, *African Designs from Traditional Sources.*

� C O N T E N T S खखख

Comrades of Color Caucus leaders relax at the 1993 Freedom Socialist Party Convention. Back row (left to right): Ann Rogers, Gil Veyna, Nancy Reiko Kato, Merle Woo. Front row (left to right): Nellie Wong, Moisés Montoya, Debra O'Gara, Yolanda Alaniz, Emily Woo Yamasaki.

⚅⚅ INTRODUCTION ⚅⚅

I n your hands is a treasure: a compilation of 14 years of writings on a rich array of subjects by activists of color in the Freedom Socialist Party (FSP) and Radical Women (RW).

With our written words, we have traversed racial, ethnic, and sexual boundaries in giving voice to our true selves, drawing on our life experiences with many forms of oppression. Our writings give volume to voices which have long been silenced, distorted or ignored.

We are members of the National Comrades of Color Caucus (NCCC) of the Freedom Socialist Party and Radical Women. We are African American, Chicana/o, Latina/o, indigenous people, and Asian Pacific Americans of Chinese, Korean, Japanese and Filipino ancestry. Our ranks include lesbians, gays, straights, youth, elders, workers, and students. We are integrationist, internationalist, feminist and multi-issue.

We believe that people of color will spearhead the coming American revolution. We know the forefront role of people of color is fundamental to reaching a new day without the human degradation and other horrors of capitalism. We have joined forces with our allies to create that new day of freedom.

This anthology is a labor of love and our gift to you, our readers, and to ourselves—a gift which expresses our belief in the beauty of the struggle for social change and the possibility of creating a better world.

Our voices

Articles in this collection were originally published between 1982-97 in the "Voices of Color" column of the *Freedom Socialist* newspaper, a regular and still continuing feature coordinated by the National Comrades of Color Caucus. Topics include an analysis of tensions between African Americans and Jews, the heroism of Black feminists, the fortitude of Chinese immigrants, the labor struggles of Chicanas/Chicanos, the dehumanization of Asians and Pacific Islanders, the ongoing sovereignty battles of indigenous people, the courageous fight of lesbians and gays of color, the necessity for bilingualism and Ethnic Studies programs, and much more.

The book also contains guest articles on Jewish issues. Periodically we have asked our Jewish colleagues to contribute pieces for the "Voices of Color" column on subjects such as the role of Jewish radicals in the antiwar movement and the need for a socialist, anti-Zionist solution in Palestine. While anti-Semitism differs from racism in its historic roots and modern expression, we feel a bond with workingclass Jews due to our shared experiences of discrimination and the laudable part played by Jews in the '60s Black civil rights movement and other progressive struggles. Given today's heightened climate of anti-Semitism, we feel it is especially important for people of color to speak out against the oppression of Jews.

As a whole, these writings are intended to promote ongoing discussions in people of color communities and on the Left. We also hope to encourage our brothers and sisters of color to get acquainted with Radical Women and the Freedom Socialist Party and join us in becoming agents for revolutionary progress.

Who we are

The National Comrades of Color Caucus is unique in the history of the Left. And so are the parent groups to which we belong.

The Freedom Socialist Party and its sister group, Radical Women, are multiracial, revolutionary feminist organizations. We believe that the most exploited—in particular women of color—have the potential to unite and guide a worldwide movement that can win total human liberation through the overthrow of capitalist rule. The FSP is a 30-year-old political party of women and men in the living tradition of Marx, Engels, Lenin and Trotsky. Radical Women is an autonomous women's organization dedicated to developing female leaders and providing a leftwing direction to the feminist movement.

The NCCC is composed of the people of color within both organizations. National Coordinator Yolanda Alaniz has headed the NCCC for many years, overseeing the growth of national leadership and caucuses in Los Angeles, New York, San Francisco and Seattle. We are a thriving body of thinkers and doers, vindicating the FSP and RW program of the key role of the most oppressed and putting forth our ideas as radicals of color.

The main purposes of the NCCC are to use tough love—supportive criticism and, just as important, praise—to shape a cohesive team of strong individuals; to assess the state of race liberation efforts; to direct the intervention of RW and FSP in the people of color movements; and to monitor our organizations to insure that problems regarding race are expeditiously and fairly resolved.

The caucus analyzes current issues and arrives at courses of action. We practice what we think, taking our ideas and energies into our communities, where we educate about the need to join forces against all oppression.

We participate in every aspect of FSP and RW life. Together, we build united fronts to stop the Nazis. We defend abortion rights and fight forced sterilization of women of color. We work for affirmative action and organize against discriminatory legislation. We strive for democracy and social activism in our unions and for a labor party that will break with the treacherous, big-business-controlled Democrats and Republicans. We advocate lesbian/gay/bisexual/transgender rights. We uphold the Cuban revolution and denounce the U.S. blockade against it. We support indigenous struggles in the Americas and around the world.

We share a collective belief: that workingclass people of all races, sexes, ages, and sexualities can and must work together to defeat our common and most powerful enemy —the capitalist system. We recognize that we are not each others' enemies. This unifying credo creates a foundation upon which we can construct a society without class distinctions, where all may live their lives on the highest plane of human culture.

Origin of the caucus

The National Comrades of Color Caucus was born in February 1981 out of the kind of intense political conflict that often sparks new developments in the radical move-ment. That these debates did not destroy FSP and RW, but instead strengthened them, is a tribute to these groups and to the Comrades of Color Caucus.

The role of people of color in our organizations came under scrutiny when a few white members of Radical Women formed a hostile clique in the Seattle branch. A clique is an unprincipled political alliance which promotes secondary, organizational gripes to a paramount level or raises misleading charges that disguise ideological differ-ences. Such dishonest machinations are always accompa-nied by an attack on leadership.

The 1981 grouping blasted Radical Women's stan-dards of accountability and collective decision-making and falsely accused FSP of "dominating" Radical Women. They tried to gain the support of new, inexperienced members of color by claiming RW's program was racist in advocating the vanguard role of women of color.

It was clear that the intriguers' charges of racism were in themselves a racist attempt to use the women of color.

Much to their credit, all the members of color remained loyal to Radical Women. They refused to join the antagonistic faction and stood with white members in calling the manipulators on their outrageous behavior.

Once the truth was exposed, the clique slithered away, never to be heard from again.

This short-lived crisis afforded an opportunity. The militants of color who had defended Radical Women against the clique decided to continue their out-front role by forming the Comrades of Color Caucus.

We are grateful to the late Clara Fraser—the stellar Jewish feminist cofounder of FSP and RW—for suggesting the caucus and advancing the participation of people of color in many other ways over numerous decades. Clara was often the first to recognize when attention was needed to internal race relations and to recommend intervention on race issues outside our groups. In many instances, she was at the helm in showing comrades how to confront racism and anti-Semitism and initiating action on these questions. It is a credit to FSP and RW, the organizations to which she dedicated her life, that the comrades of color are not alone in dealing with matters of race.

Another crisis strengthens the caucus

In 1991, ten years after the Seattle fight, the Comrades of Color Caucus grew to maturity after another sharp but necessary conflict within the Bay Area branch. (See "We are the leaders we've been waiting for," page 101.) This time, an attack on national FSP leadership was launched by two white females and a Black man.

Once again, accusations of racism were raised as a smokescreen: the defectors' real motivation was their refusal to be held accountable and their rejection of revolutionary politics. They seized on two unrelated incidents of insensitivity by two white members and rejected all attempts at resolution. They intended to set up the comrades of color to do their fighting for them by fomenting an internal war over race. But the comrades of color proved once again they would not be used in the name of racism as a weapon against FSP and RW.

The Bay Area's principal members of color—Nellie Wong, Moisés Montoya, Nancy Reiko Kato and Merle Woo—rallied to defend themselves, their branch, and the national party. In this, they received the full backing of comrades of color in other cities, the FSP National Office, and the entire international membership.

With courage, dedication, and *ganas* (desire), Bay Area comrades of color combatted the factionalizers. They took the offensive and victoriously reclaimed their branch. The traitors left, having failed to recruit even one adherent outside the Bay Area. Another clique went down the tube of opportunism and reformism, disgracing themselves along the way.

Lessons learned

Comrades of color received quite a political education from these battles. We vowed: Never will we be used! Never will we be tokens! And never will we allow anyone to betray our class and our program by fabricating racist incidents or by refusing to clear up real occurrences of racism. To carry out these resolves, we set ourselves the task of becoming the strongest and most confident, highly skilled and theoretically grounded leaders possible.

As human beings living under the distorted social conditions of capitalism, none of us are exempt from making racist, sexist or homophobic mistakes. We make no excuses for oppressive conduct in society or in our organizations. But we find it most effective to confront our political colleagues within the context of our common beliefs and with a calm and rational approach. The comrades of color, and the entire membership of FSP and RW, are committed to correcting racist behavior through timely, direct, open, honest, and educational discussions. Because we share a socialist ideology which upholds the highest standards of human relations, we are able to both clear up racism when it occurs and reach an understanding of its root cause.

Class war, not race war

A central issue addressed in these pages is whether fighting racism is a crucial front line in a united battle for class liberation or whether each oppressed race is engaged in a separate war against whites.

The NCCC believes it can be very valuable for people of color, especially women of color, to form their own groups and work together on shared concerns. We agree with independent organizing as long as it does not preclude participation in the multiracial struggles of working people. Such autonomous initiatives are very different from the separatist policy of cultural nationalism.

Cultural nationalists react to racism by uniting around color and culture alone and ignoring *class*—the fundamental division of society into haves and have-nots, bosses and workers. In the name of racial solidarity, they usually end up supporting members of their own ethnicity within the ruling class at the expense of workers of all colors. In addition, racial exclusivity erects a barrier between workers of other races who should be natural allies.

We understand the attraction of clustering with one's race "family" against whites. A similar response to oppression has at times generated separatism among feminists, lesbians and Jews. There are strong pressures to conform to isolationism, but it has deadly consequences.

Cultural nationalism's blindness to class makes it reactionary. It does not address the origin of racism in capitalism's drive to reap maximum profits by using bigotry to justify grossly underpaying people of color and to divide the entire working class. By wrongly identifying whites as the enemy rather than capitalism, race separatism arrives at disastrous tactics. It directs workers of color away from their allies among white workers, prevents linkages among women of different races, and leads to treacherous blocs with the bosses for the sake of a few crumbs. It denies the importance of other liberation struggles and is deeply sexist, homophobic, anti-Semitic, anti-radical, and hostile to other people of color.

Our answer as socialist feminists of color is very clear. We counter the misleaders. We educate that we are in a *class* war, not a *race* war. We refuse to play the suicidal divide-and-conquer game of people of color against each other and against whites. We unite with those who have common interests with us, no matter the color of their skin. We propose a program to bring the class together, not split it. At the same time, we fight bigotry whenever it appears and recognize that in order to stop racism or other kinds of oppression, we must defeat capitalism and replace it with socialism.

This may not be the easy way out, but it is the only way that can succeed.

¡*Viva la revolución!*

The National Comrades of Color Caucus is committed to achieving a better life for all people. We find fulfillment in collective action on all issues of equality, liberation, and self-expression. By ridding the world of prejudice and oppression, the human species will not simply survive, but will flourish.

It is with this purpose that we continue to speak our minds in the "Voices of Color" column and in every other arena. Enjoy the fruits of our labor.

YOLANDA ALANIZ
NCCC National Coordinator
Los Angeles, California

NELLIE WONG
Bay Area FSP Organizer
San Francisco, California

Third World Conference of Lesbians and Gays: The personal vs. political

1982

by Yolanda Alaniz

T he first time that Third World lesbians and gays met for a national conference was a political high for everyone. That was in October 1979, and 500 people engaged in an intensive debate of political ideas, points of unity, and differences. Afterwards, the conference became an impressive contingent in a massive march on Washington, D.C. held that same weekend.

By comparison, the second national conference in Chicago on Thanksgiving weekend 1981 was a downer, a disappointment.

Poor advance publicity, travel difficulties posed by the air traffic controllers' strike, and a hefty registration fee combined to keep attendance below a hundred.

The conference agenda primarily addressed personal feelings and relationships, and individual solutions. Despite a banner proclaiming "A Unified Rainbow of Strength," the focus was not on program or organizing, but on forming networks for individual contacts.

Daniel Tsang, conference speaker and editor of *Gay Insurgent,* had something important to say: "Our challenge is to form a united front against our oppressor." These fighting words could have sparked productive discussion had the conference organizers, the National

Coalition of Black Gays, wanted it and planned for it. But they didn't.

Conference organizers took no political responsibility or leadership for the conference itself or the movement as a whole. They let the conference flounder aimlessly, without purpose or direction.

Sparks of life

Despite the anti-political atmosphere, there were encouraging signs of forward political movement. Given the opportunity for debate in a few workshops, many people eagerly discussed the state of the lesbian/gay movement and related political issues.

Tom Boot of the Freedom Socialist Party led the workshop "A Left Wing Perspective on Radical Politics, Lesbian/Gay Liberation, and Race." He pointed out that many liberals are more afraid of radicals than of the right wing, and ally themselves with the oppressors.

Radical Women member Bird Wilson told the workshop that the FSP and RW are socialist feminist organiza-

tions that see the leadership of the lesbian/gay movement—especially the leadership of women of color—as decisive to the American revolution.

Said Wilson, "Lesbians of color are at the bottom of each social movement, and this social and economic oppression puts us in a key position to be the strongest fighters. We have the least to lose and the most to gain. We are unique because as women, women of color, lesbians, and workers, we combine all the issues and movements."

The workshop passed a resolution calling on workers, the oppressed, and radicals to build a united front against the right wing. When this was brought before the conference's final assembly it passed overwhelmingly.

Labor party debate

At this final session, a resolution supporting a labor party was cosponsored by the Revolutionary Workers League and the Freedom Socialist Party. Both are Trotskyist organizations whose members work in many political arenas, including the lesbian/gay movement.

The resolution exposed the dependence of the Democratic and Republican parties on the capitalist class, and called for the formation of a labor party so that working people can wage an independent fight for political power instead of scrambling after the phantom concessions offered by the major parties.

The resolution was defeated by a small margin, but only after stimulating and energetic debate.

Defense of Woo and Wong

A resolution in defense of socialist feminist poets Merle Woo and Nellie Wong was also hotly debated.

Both women have come under attack in the movement press for their politics, sex, and race.

Unfortunately, some men attendees said they lacked enough information to support both women, and amended the resolution to challenge only a single attack on Woo in *Midwest* magazine. The conference passed the amended version and agreed to write *Midwest* to protest its racist, anti-feminist, dehumanizing editorial against Woo, and to support radicals' right to speak out.

Forward or backward

Despite its organizers, many conference participants proved that there is still hunger for political discussion, growth, and action within the lesbian/gay movement. In just 11 months, Reagan's administration has wiped out major historic gains for civil rights, labor, and the disadvantaged, and a new radicalism is being born.

But the important questions remain: Will the National Coalition of Black Gays and other Third World lesbian/gay groups take the initiative to meet the challenge? Will we confront not only racism but its vicious tentacles of sexism, homophobia, and class exploitation? Will we sit back or fight?

Personal escape is impossible—and suicidal. To survive, we must resist, not disappear into narcissism. Nobody else is going to do our work for us. We either organize and struggle or we retreat to the closet and get stampeded into the concentration camps. Let's stand up for life.

Campesina's journey

1982

by Yolanda Alaniz

I was raised in Eastern Washington's Yakima Valley, a fertile, rich, and beautiful farming region known to Chicanos as the Little Mississippi of the Northwest because of the local racism against Chicanos.

My family were *campesinos*—migrant farmworkers—who settled in Sunnyside, the heart of the region. Most people there are Chicano.

My mother worked in the fields to support her five kids. I had to work in the fields before and after school every day, plus weekends from sunup to sundown, to help the family. I remember the poverty: the farm labor camps where we lived had no electricity or running water, and our community outhouse was in the center of the camp.

At school, our culture and language were denied us. We were not allowed to learn Chicano history. Our teachers favored the white students and fanned their racism against us. I'll never forget white kids laughing at me for bringing *tortillas con papas* for lunch and for wearing secondhand clothes and shoes.

Our teachers weren't there to educate, but to funnel all Chicanos into relatively unskilled jobs. They told me to forget about college and to seek jobs where I could use my hands, which I was "used to."

By the time I graduated from high school, only a handful of Chicanos were left. The rest had been forced to drop out and go to work, were expelled, or had been so discouraged by racism that they quit.

As I walked down the aisle to get my diploma, I felt so proud of myself and *mi mamá,* who had pushed me to finish school. Only two out of the seven children and step-children in my family graduated from high school. And I was the only one to finish college.

La raza unida

In September 1969, I moved to Seattle to attend the University of Washington under the Equal Opportunity Program, which allowed minority and poor students to make up college-prep deficiencies, and provided federal loans and scholarships.

It was a very good year in which to begin my higher education. The Chicano movement had erupted with a vengeance in the wake of the Black civil rights struggles and amid the protests against the Vietnam War.

Campus was *hot* with political activity. I was very quickly transformed from a "Mexican American" into a *Chicana* political activist, like so many others.

It was Chicanos against the world!

We needed everything! We demanded everything! And we had a *right* to everything!

Our number one enemy was the gringo, just like back home. Our allies were ourselves. Our tactics were militant: demonstrate, rally, take the building! We demanded Chicano studies, Chicano classes, radical professors, more financial aid, no sellouts. We went off campus, took to the streets, organized contingents in the antiwar demos.

We wanted it all. And I loved every minute of it!

Race is primary?

The time was right for winning some demands. But fights soon broke out among the different peoples of color over who was going to get a bigger share of the pie.

It took us awhile to realize we weren't each other's

enemies. The gringo was. So we formed alliances with one another. Still, we Chicanos always held that the Chicano struggle was foremost. Race was the primary issue. And Chicano culture, regardless of class or political differences, was the basis of our unity and strength. Our slogan was *Chicano Power!*

For many, this was a self-affirming expression of pride, long overdue after centuries of degradation.

For others, however, Chicano Power led to cultural separatism and the belief that one's own people were superior to all others. These were the cultural nationalists, and they became dominant in the Chicano movement.

I was no separatist, but I believed that only Chicanos could fight Chicano oppression and that being Chicano was all that mattered in the struggle. I also felt that unity among all people of color would be forthcoming in any showdown with the gringos.

Three developments changed my perspective.

I saw that the sexism of the macho leaders of MEChA, the leading Chicano student organization, was rapidly pushing women out of the movement. And it soon became clear that the "race is primary" viewpoint made it impossible to address sexism.

Secondly, I saw that elevating one's own culture above all others led to friction between people of color and lessened our joint effectiveness against the powers-that-be.

Finally, I learned how quickly class and political divisions take precedence over race or ethnic unity. A Black UW administrator fired the director of the Chicano division of Minority Affairs because of the latter's involvement in the movement!

Race and culture politics were getting us nowhere fast. But I had no alternative.

¡Hola, revolución!

Looking back, I was lucky that I had to work my way through college. Otherwise, I might never have become involved in a campus labor struggle that changed my life.

This fight was in opposition to a sexist and racist job reclassification system that would have lowered pay scales for entry-level jobs and clerical, service, and other low-paid positions, the bulk of which were filled by women and people of color.

I wound up helping to organize United Workers Union-Independent, which fought for the most oppressed workers at the university.

Seattle Radical Women members were in the leadership of this union. And in working with them, I learned for the first time to trust white workers on the basis of *political agreement.*

Something else happened: I found new strength and commitment to struggle through the support and political leadership of these socialist women. And my own deeply suppressed feminism emerged.

This was something *really* new! I was learning how to fight simultaneously against my oppression as a Chicana, a woman, a worker, and a mother. I felt for the first time that I was fighting for *all* of what I am and who I am.

This was socialist feminism. And it was for *me!*

It wasn't long, however, before I was told to stay a- **I was learning to fight against my oppression as a Chicana, a woman, a worker, and a mother.** way from Radical Women by the Chicana culturalists and the sexist Chicano men. Then my husband gave me a further ultimatum: "Be my full-time wife. I don't want a political wife."

My decision was clear. *Adiós mi esposo,* good morning independence!

I joined Radical Women. And soon I joined the Freedom Socialist Party, the only revolutionary feminist party on earth. It had to be.

Adiós to Aztlán

My subsequent work in the Chicano community often brought me in conflict with those same cultural nationalists who had tried to drive me out of the movement. They were still in the leadership and still shouting out anti-gringo separatism as the solution to our oppression.

Our own nation—Aztlán—was their war cry. But how this nation would be achieved, where it would be located, and how its current inhabitants would be removed, they never said.

I couldn't buy it. The U.S. government had forced segregation on us for hundreds of years. Why voluntarily go along with that program? Why remove ourselves as a challenge to the segregation, exploitation, discrimination, and genocide of U.S. rule? What could this self-imposed segregation into a new capitalist country possibly gain us?

This is not to say that my culture is not important to me—it is. But my culture is far *more* than just a slogan for macho self-aggrandizement. I will not use it to hide myself from struggle and to yearn for an unreachable—and undesirable!—Aztlán.

We Chicanas and Chicanos are the victims of racism, treated like foreigners and relegated to second- and third-class citizenship. Yet the USA is *our* land. We are Americans.

My people have been here for 400 years. We were once Mexicanos, part of Mexico, but almost 150 years have passed since our land was ripped away from Mexico by the gringos. And our culture has grown away from Mexico, taking much from the Indian, the Black, and the Anglo. Indeed, we call ourselves Chicano in acknowledgment of our Indian blood. We are who we are today in relation to all the other cultures we lived beside and commingled with through the years.

Our culture is uniquely our own. But culture is not enough to form a nation. We do not have our own economy, and ownership of the economy is basic to nationhood. Also, our territory is shared with many other peoples. These factors make a separate nation impossible.

We are workers, part of the U.S. proletariat. Our labor *built* the American Southwest. Driven off our land and herded into *barrios,* we worked in the mines, on railroads and on ranches, and in factories. Our blood and sweat have been incorporated into the muscle and bone of the U.S. economy.

We are workers who keep this country running. This country is ours. We earned it. And we are not about to leave it. Our job is to *transform* it.

¡Viva la revolución Americana!

It is as workers, fighting together with our sisters and brothers of all colors against the bosses, that we Chicanos proudly take our place as leaders in the American revolution.

Who knows better than we, the super-oppressed, how to fight and defeat our real enemy, the U.S. capitalist class—those sexists, racists, exploiters, dividers, and oppressors of people of color, women, children, gays, and every worker?

We are warriors in a class conflagration. We have fought with other American workers for survival and dignity as workers against bosses and cops and the government. We Chicanos organized and led countless unions; we imparted to U.S. unionism the fiery idealism and socialist theory of the Mexican Revolution.

I take my stand in the American revolution as a socialist and a feminist fighting for a place in the sun and a better life for Chicanos and for all of us.

¡Adelante mujer!
¡Viva el socialismo y la libertad!

Exploring common differences

1983

by Nellie Wong

I can just hear my mother now. "What do you mean, *you're* going to a conference of international women of color? You mean *you're* going to speak—and to read poetry, too?"

Unfortunately, my mother's gone and doesn't know I've become a poet and socialist feminist activist. If she were here, you can bet our conversations would be peppered with excitement. Our mouths would taste the curry of talk among women of color. And I'd have a heck of a time explaining in Cantonese American English just what I'd be saying at this conference called "Common Differences: Third World Women and Feminist Perspectives."

To explore the complex similarities and differences among 600 women from diverse groups and cultures! To read, to write, and speak out. Just up my alley. The conference was a whirlwind. Who slept? Not this long steam lady, this *cheong hay poa,* loquacious woman.

The conference was held from April 9-13, 1983 at the University of Illinois. Agenda topics ranged from cross-cultural perspectives on feminism, to women in revolutionary movements, to the politics of women's health and reproductive rights, to racism and sexism in popular culture. Panelists and participants included Native American, Asian/Pacific, Chicana/Latina, and Black women of the U.S., and women from Latin America, Africa, Asia,

Europe, and the Middle East. We met and heard key-noters Isabel Letelier from Chile, Dr. Nawal el Sadaawi from Egypt, and Ntozake Shange and Cherríe Moraga of the United States.

The world's women spoke on the world of problems and oppression we face—the growing poverty of women, hungry children, the plight of refugees. But hardly anyone named our common enemy: international capitalism, which maintains racism, sexism, and heterosexism to keep women down.

Academic excellence and scholarship were the cuisine at this conference. But we in Radical Women had a spicy dish to serve—worldwide socialist feminism, the theory and action that flow from our lives. We stressed solidarity among all the exploited; the political leadership of women of color, lesbians, workers and feminist men; building a socialist feminist revolution on U.S. soil.

Out of the shadows

Even at this gathering, the myth of Asian American invisibility shrouded us. Very few Asian/Pacific women from the U.S. or other countries attended. There were no workshops or panels to deal with our issues. We had to fight to be seen and heard.

We organized our own workshop to address this invisibility, this racism. Our speakers included Susie Ling from L.A., Emily Woo Yamasaki and Christine Choy of New York City, Lola Wing from Chicago, and me, from Oakland, California.

Over 50 people came, many of us Asian/Pacific Americans. Where did everybody suddenly come from? We talked about stereotyped images of Asian/Pacific women, prostitution, lesbianism, feminism, and free speech.

My comrade, Emily Woo Yamasaki, hit hard at the problem of invisibility which, she said, "extends into politics, too." At Isabel Letelier's keynote address, Emily had said that "the best way we in the United States can support struggle abroad is to have a revolution here." Some people laughed! "People looked at me as a young Asian woman and didn't take me seriously—I needed to 'grow out of it.' To these people I say: *you* are the ones who have to come to terms with reality."

Emily, who represented New York Radical Women and the Merle Woo Defense Committee at the conference, got a resolution passed at this workshop supporting Merle Woo, who was fired from her job at the University of California at Berkeley because of her feminism, lesbianism, and radical politics.

Ma, I wish you could have seen us carrying out the lessons you taught about being prepared, speaking out, and fighting to win.

The artist and politics

If my mother had been at the conference, she would have heard me speak on the unity of poetry and principled activism at a panel about women and language.

"If we choose to write about women's work and struggles in non-personal terms, we are being rhetorical, not universal—boring, unfeminine, whatever. And if we write personally, about having to be on welfare, or being afraid our husbands will take our children because we're lesbians or revolutionaries, or if we write other than 'standard' American English—whatever that is—then indeed we have violated the 'acceptable' code of literature.

"But I seek the words and the language of the most militant fighters for freedom. I seek the beauty of human struggle, to sing out what our foremothers and forefathers fought for, to give inspiration, love and support to those people who are still fighting for bread and roses."

A heated and healthy debate

A hidden dispute raged throughout the conference between cultural feminists, who advocated lesbianism as a single-issue solution to women's oppression, and homophobic Stalinist academics, who pushed class and race as the primary issues, defining lesbianism as a personal, secondary issue.

This debate burst into the open near the end of the conference, after a keynote address by Chicana lesbian writer Cherríe Moraga. Her exclusive emph-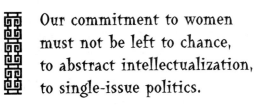 **Our commitment to women must not be left to chance, to abstract intellectualization, to single-issue politics.** asis on lesbianism started a heated—and healthy —debate on the floor. But Moraga's response was to halt discussion, turn off the mike, and leave the room!

Our ideas as women of color were thus censored. Those of us who saw the synthesis of race, class, sex, and sexual oppression—with none "secondary"—had no chance to speak.

Yet this explosion prompted those who had been pushing for political action at the conference to go to the mikes in the wake of Moraga's departure and organize on the spot for preparing and passing resolutions. As a result, the final plenary *did* take political stands, against the intentions of the conference organizers. The vote was unanimous for a resolution supporting Merle Woo, and for another which called for making lesbianism and sexuality central issues for discussion at future conferences.

Heads and tails

What can I say about this conference as a whole?

My father would have criticized it as *yew how, mo mee.* Have head, no tail. We must extend feminist politics to *yew how, yew mee.* Have head, have tail. The *whole* body, mind *and* action. Militant politics which embrace the personal and art.

Our political commitment to women internationally must not be left to chance, to abstract intellectualization, to single-issue politics, to elevating the struggle against racism over the fight against sexism, to opportunism.

We must learn the wisdom of survival which our parents knew. My parents, who raised seven children in Oakland Chinatown, three of us born in China, had to pay attention to details, plan for tomorrow.

I, the first U.S.-born daughter, know that among our common differences we must find a common understanding, a unity that will lead us to liberation.

Lesbians of Color Conference: The politics of "sisterhood"

1983

by Nancy Reiko Kato

"Sisters Bonding" was the theme for the first national Lesbians of Color Conference, held September 8-11, 1983 in Malibu, California. Over 200 women of color, among them Latinas, Chicanas, Asian Americans, Native Americans, Blacks, and Caribbean women, attended. They included lesbian separatists, leftists, and independents. The radical wing of the lesbian/gay movement was represented by Seattle's Stonewall Committee for Lesbian/Gay Rights. Socialist feminists also attended, represented by National Radical Women.

Los Angeles Lesbians of Color organized the conference so that "we may begin to know each other, reach out, touch and trust, to form lasting alliances and friendship..." Unfortunately, what they had in mind were primarily personal and social, rather than political, alliances.

There is nothing at all wrong with getting to know each other. But at a time when lesbians of color desperately need to mount national strategies to fight against everything from anti-abortion attacks to gaybashing to social service cuts to repressive immigration legislation to union busting, getting to know each other is not enough.

This conference had great potential as a starting point for strategizing and organizing against rightwing reaction. But it shortchanged those women who came for serious political discussion and active proposals for fighting back that they could take home to their communities.

Most of the workshops were aimed in an anti-political direction, dealing with things such as personal identity, spirituality, and self-growth. A visible portion of conference attendees came merely to have a good time and to develop social networks. They wanted their own space—to retreat from political commitment.

Anti-political politics

But there is no real retreat from politics, or from the racism, sexism, and class oppression that permeate capitalist society, including the movements for social change. The anti-political atmosphere at the conference actually gave rise to two very definite brands of political ideology, lesbian separatism and cultural nationalism, both of which express capitulation to racist and sexist divisiveness and thrive in an atmosphere of political retreat.

Separatism and cultural nationalism are *exclusionary* by nature. Separatists see men—and straight women—as the enemy. Cultural nationalists see culture and color as the only bases for interaction and alliance. Both attack all those who do not look, think, or act like they do.

There were two groups of women who came under fire from the separatists and cultural nationalists at the conference: straight women of color with long histories of solidarity with the lesbian/gay movement, who'd been invited by the conference organizers to give workshops, and light-skinned lesbians, who weren't colored enough to suit the nationalists.

Straight-baiting started at a meeting called on the second day to discuss issues which weren't being addressed at the conference. A separatist jumped up and proclaimed that she didn't "want anything to do with a woman who plugs into a man." Cultural nationalists also attacked the light-skinned lesbians present. Not surprisingly, both they and the separatists *opposed* discussing the issues of racism, sexism, and class oppression in society and what can be done to end them. One remarked that she had come to the conference to get away from all that.

Defending our allies

A majority of the women at the meeting defended the right of straight and light-skinned women to attend. One Latina stated, "We must be *inclusive*, not exclusive." Radical Women member Merle Woo pointed out that many straight women have given unwavering support to lesbian and gay rights at the expense of being unmercifully lesbian-baited themselves. Woo pointed to fellow RW member Nellie Wong, a nationally known poet who has consistently defended lesbian/gay rights in her art. Wong, she said, like the other straight women at the conference, is an ally to be welcomed rather than repudiated.

As a result of the attacks, Radical Women members—Woo, Wong, and Nancy Kato from the Bay Area, Emily Woo Yamasaki from New York City, and Midge Ward from Seattle, a Native American activist who also represented the Stonewall Committee—drafted a resolution that excoriated:

> ...the divisive and self-destructive politics based on sexuality and skin color.
>
> We could have endless discussions of who a REAL lesbian of color is and never get around to setting about fighting the real enemy. Some lesbians of color are looking for a safe space, thinking safety is where we are all the same. But in reality, safety is where we can unite with others to defeat the right wing, capitalism, and the patriarchy. Safety is not obtained by shutting out our allies.

Where the action was

Despite the separatists, cultural nationalists, and the general anti-political tenor of the conference, there were a few sessions that included good political discussions that struck a note of reality in dealing with the oppression of lesbians of color.

A statement from the Indian Women's Circle, which focused on the genocide against Native people, called on lesbians of color to support Indian women's leadership in the social change movements and demanded the right to self-determination for Native Americans. Also, the Open Rap Group for Asian Lesbians proposed 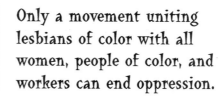 **Only a movement uniting lesbians of color with all women, people of color, and workers can end oppression.** compiling an Asian lesbian anthology and presenting a panel on Asian lesbians at the next National Women's Studies Association Conference.

Nellie Wong gave a workshop entitled "The Battle to Overcome Racism in the Women's Movement." Almost a quarter of the women at the conference sat in to hear Wong stress the importance of women of color and white women uniting to fight against the color line in the feminist movement. Wong emphasized the importance of confronting racism inside the movement and said that white women have a special responsibility to fight it. She stated, however, that racism, like sexism, cannot be fought on an individual basis and that only a movement uniting lesbians of color with all women, people of color, and the entire working class can make the political, social, and economic changes necessary to end our oppression.

Another workshop, entitled "Politics: Knowing and Acting," featured talks by Merle Woo, who was fired from the University of California/Berkeley for being a lesbian and a socialist feminist; Kwambe OmDahda, a lawyer and founder of Lesbians of Color; and Mitsuye Yamada, a teacher and poet who is co-featured in the film *Mitsuye and Nellie: Asian American Poets*.

Woo explained that her fight to regain her job is both a direct challenge to the political discrimination perpetrated at UC and "a way of educating people about multi-issue, socialist feminist ideas." OmDahda gave a good presentation on the legal rights of lesbians, and Yamada stressed the importance of grassroot struggles.

A resolution in support of Woo's case was passed in this workshop. Unfortunately, there was no place on the agenda for formal resolutions to be adopted by the conference as a whole—a result of the organizers' refusal to take political responsibility for the lesbians of color movement.

Real ties that bind

There are some hard political lessons to be learned from this conference, and a need for continued discussion on sexual and color politics in our communities.

We can only hope that the bankrupt politics of lesbian separatism and cultural nationalism will be totally rejected from our movement, that never again will the separatists and nationalists be allowed to launch shameless attacks on light-skinned lesbians and the straight women of color who stand with us, and that bonding between sisters will be based on a movement that *unites* us in the fight to end our oppression.

Medgar Evers College: Shall education serve the community?

1984

by Emily Woo Yamasaki

I n this era of rampant cutbacks in education, the fight by students, faculty, and staff to save Medgar Evers College (MEC) in Brooklyn, New York gives heart to the nationwide struggle to make education serve the needs of the community.

Located in the largest Black community in the Western Hemisphere, Medgar Evers College was established in 1971 as a result of demands by New York City's Black community for an "experimental and innovative institution which meets the needs of the city it must serve." The college is one of 17 in the City University of New York (CUNY) system. Ninety-five percent of its 3,000 students are Black, 73% are women, two-thirds of them mothers.

From MEC's beginning, there were battles with administration over its direction. The first came in 1972 when students attempted to oust MEC President Richard Trent, who, though Black, willingly served the interests of the racist and sexist CUNY administration. During his tenure, Trent attempted to suppress academic freedom through intimidation and harassment, and opposed Black Studies and campus childcare. In 1974, attempts by CUNY to close the college provoked clashes between police and a student/faculty coalition.

When New York hit the fiscal skids in the mid-1970s, Medgar Evers College became a prime target for budget cuts. In 1976, it was reduced from a four-year college to a two-year community college. Funding and curriculum were cut, library resources were reduced, and faculty workloads were doubled.

The campus shrank from nine buildings to two: a former warehouse and a decaying 100-year-old high school building. Heating and plumbing were unreliable. The buildings were infested with rats. CUNY figured that if it couldn't tame the students and faculty, it would let the college fall down about them.

Sitting in for equal education

As the unwanted stepchild of the CUNY system, MEC would certainly have been closed had not students and faculty fought like hell for over 10 years to keep it open. Black feminists formed the backbone of this effort.

In April 1982, following a two-week student strike, the Student-Faculty-Community-Alumni Coalition to Save Medgar Evers College initiated an historic 110-day sit-in in President Trent's office, which finally forced him to resign.

The sit-in also won a drop-in childcare center and a Center for Women's Development. But funding was not forthcoming.

Presidential politics

Retaliation followed close on the heels of these victories. Trent's CUNY-appointed successor, Acting President Dennis Paul, denied reappointment to four professors who were active members of the Coalition. Only rapid mobilization by an angry community won back all four jobs.

Not learning from that lesson, Paul axed five more progressive faculty members in December 1983, his last month in office. Four of the teachers were women and all had excellent academic standing. These firings were clearly designed to eliminate opposition to Paul's perma-

One of many community protests over the years to preserve Medgar Evers College.

nent appointment as MEC's president, and also to thwart development of a Black Studies program. One target, Dr. Sheila Mayers-Johnson, was the country's first chairperson of a Black Studies program.

Undaunted, the Coalition stepped up its campaign for community control of the college. At a series of CUNY Board of Trustees meetings in the fall of '83, students, faculty, and supporters from community and feminist organizations demanded that the permanent president be a Black woman who understood the students' needs. They called for restoration of MEC to four-year senior college status, adequate funding for the Child Development Center Studies program, and repair of college facilities.

Despite student and faculty advocacy of a Black woman progressive, Dr. Gloria Joseph, the CUNY chancellor and trustees picked a Black man, Jay Carrington Chunn, for president.

At first, Chunn appeared to support the activists. He

rehired three of the five fired professors. He appointed several women to the position of dean. And he lobbied to have Medgar Evers College restored to four-year status.

But these moves were designed to lull the community to sleep, and Chunn has now reneged on his earlier promises of funding and support. An especially sharp battle is shaping up over Chunn's refusal to fund needed counseling and secretarial positions for the Women's Center. The Center's staff and supporters have demanded a meeting with Chunn, and MEC's faculty voted to boycott his official November 8 inauguration.

Back to battle

It's a new school year and back to the fight for the heirs of Medgar Evers in Brooklyn's Black community, especially the intransigent Black women who lead the MEC fight and rally to it all those concerned with equal education and equal rights.

The MEC struggle shows once again that we can't expect equal educational opportunity from CUNY-like bureaucracies, but only through shared, persistent, and militant community commitment to the aspirations of the oppressed. The determined Black women and their supporters will prevail at Medgar Evers College.

Women strikers shake up the Bay Area

1985

by Nancy Reiko Kato

In the San Francisco Bay Area, constant strike activity marked the 50th anniversary of the 1934 San Francisco General Strike. But in 50 years, the face of organized labor has dramatically changed. The primary impetus for the 1934 strike came from white males in unions such as the longshoremen's union; people of color and women were denied entry into many jobs; and, in addition, many unions had discriminatory policies that barred them from membership. Today it is women of color who are the driving force in Bay Area labor actions; although racism and sexism have kept them in low-paid, "unskilled" jobs, they have entered the work force in ever-growing numbers and have been the strongest fighters for unionization.

This is not just a local phenomenon but part of a nationwide labor resurgence spearheaded by people of color, who, while historically leaders in battles for workers' rights, have only in the last decades gained a foothold within organized labor. The most shunned and exploited workers now far outnumber relatively privileged white males in the work force. And women of color, trained as fighters by their life struggles against bigotry and poverty, are the staunchest of fighters who resist because they *must*.

Over the past year, Filipinas, Chicanas/Latinas,

Chinese and Black women have struck Bay Area companies that seek to weaken and bust trade unions and crush labor unrest with take-away contracts carrying drastic wage and health benefit cuts, and with two-tier wage systems that pay new hires less than other workers.

Many of the strikes are still being fought. Others have been concluded successfully. Still others have been busted by the bosses, with the collusion of union bureaucrats.

Fighting the onslaught

When the Shoreline South Intermediate Care Hospital in Alameda was sold in 1984, the new owners, in a blatant attempt to bust the union, fired 51 of the 60 members of Hospital and Institutional Workers Local 250. The workers, mostly older Black women who had worked at Shoreline for 15 to 20 years, went on strike in November 1984. Now, almost a year later, they are still out and on the picket line *seven days a week!* They demand continued recognition of the union despite changes in ownership.

On June 19, 1985, the regional office of the Reagan-dominated National Labor Relations Board rejected the union's charges that the hospital had committed race and sex discrimination in the firings. Local 250 plans to appeal to the national NLRB office. Given the strong anti-labor bias of that agency, the union must *immediately* organize a labor and community pressure campaign to force the board to make a just decision. Workers, meanwhile, continue to picket the hospital.

In San Francisco, Local 2 of the Hotel and Restaurant Employees and Bartenders Union voted overwhelmingly to strike against take-backs in September 1984. The local's membership is 50% people of color and primarily female. They voted subsequently by another large margin to *stay* on strike. Their militancy was such that it sparked discussion in the San Francisco Labor Council of calling a possible citywide general strike. Frightened by this kind of talk, Local 2 bureaucrats ended the strike in December by okaying a take-back contract the membership had earlier voted to reject. The officials also denigrated the sacrifices made by strikers for four months by agreeing in the settlement to pay $100,000 out of *union funds* for scabs' salaries!

This strike brought into clearest focus the conflicting roles and aspirations of the low-paid rank-and-file militants and the labor bureaucrats. Manifest was the enormous potential power of the strikers to ignite the entire work force in united action against the bosses. No less clear was the bureaucrats' determination to curry favor with management by squelching such action, maintaining labor "peace," and preserving the bosses' profits.

Sold out

The rank-and-file women have been sold out by their supposed leaders time and time again. The Mission Foods strike is a classic example.

Located in Richmond, Mission Foods is the only unionized tortilla factory in California. On July 5, 1984, it was struck by Hotel and Restaurant Employees and Bartenders Union Local 28, whose membership is predominantly Spanish-speaking Chicanas and Latinas who have worked at Mission Foods for over 10 years. Fighting against an *average* 30% wage cut and elimination of benefits, the women organized community support for a boycott of Mission Foods products and kept round-the-clock picket lines going at the factory.

Local 28 officials did nothing to promote the strike. But community supporters and Chicano students from the University of California at Berkeley set up a strike support committee which organized a series of community rallies to support and publicize the strike. Their call for public support also brought a massive response from unionists, including Chicano labor leader César Chávez, who joined them on the picket line. The picket—a noisy, roving line at a succession of Bay Area supermarkets—convinced store managers to remove Mission's products from their shelves.

Alarmed by the fervor of the strikers and their supporters, Local 28 officials decided to ram through management's take-away contract. They refused to provide a translator when they presented the contract proposal to the membership—*and they allowed scabs to vote on the proposal.* The contract was "ratified" in February 1985. Some workers have refused to go back under these conditions and are considering a renewed boycott against Mission. Chicano students, appalled at the union's racism and lack of democracy, are continuing their support.

Irreconcilable interests

Nationwide, the gulf between the labor bureaucracy and the rank and file is widening as union officials capitulate to the bosses' unionbusting and take-backs. The bureaucracy has become the safeguard of *business* interests, rather than an advocate for labor. Based on the privileged white male labor aristocracy, which has traded class consciousness for economic rewards, union bureaucrats foster the racism and sexism that have historically split apart the working class and allowed the capitalists to remain in power. Union officials feather their nests quite nicely under the system that profits from the exploitation of workers. Primarily concerned with carrying out the bosses' wishes, they view the militance of people of color, women, and immigrant workers as a threat they must crush if they are to retain their control and privilege.

The AFL-CIO leadership has supported the Simpson-Mazzoli bill and other racist anti-immigration legislation aimed at controlling and curtailing the rights of dark-skinned immigrant workers as well as intensifying repression against people of color in general. Its "Buy American" campaign pits U.S. workers against foreign workers and engenders violence against Asian Americans.

The demoralizing, divisive racism and sexism of the labor skates is the biggest roadblock that must be overcome to prevent the destruction of *all* labor's hard-won gains.

New life for labor

Women of color workers, who are of *necessity* leading labor's resistance against the bosses *and* the bureaucrats, are charting a course that the entire labor movement must follow if it is to stop the anti-labor offensive. Their courageous fight inspires workers who have been disillusioned by the unending round of givebacks, and shows the strength of a united struggle.

Privileged workers must in their own interest reject the poison of race and sex bigotry. Their future lies in their ability to unite with the rest of their class to stop the wholesale destruction of labor's already eroded rights. White male workers must join women and people of color in pressing their demands in the union as on the picket line. To do otherwise is to play into the hands of the bosses and be defeated without a battle.

The survival of the American labor movement lies in its ability to reject the divide-and-conquer of racism and sexism promoted by the parasitic union bureaucracy. When labor learns to respect and follow the leadership of women of color—the most oppressed and thus the most steadfast fighters—it will cast off its misleaders and be on the road to the decisive defeat of the bosses. *Then* we will see the spirit of the 1934 General Strike reborn with a power never seen before!

Year of the Dragon: An actor's dilemma

1986

by Emily Woo Yamasaki

C ountless people—actors and non-actors—dream of being in a Hollywood movie. But for an actor, there's more than the thrill of seeing yourself up there on the silver screen. To be cast in a major production is a prestigious acknowledgment of your abilities. This certainly motivated me to take part in the recent film *Year of the Dragon.*

But *Dragon* posed a terrible, ongoing conflict for me and the hundreds of other Asian Americans who worked in the film. How are we to be actors when the only roles available are in movies that stereotype, insult, or scapegoat Asian Americans, or in commercials about "Oriental" frozen foods?

Reel reality

Very few Hollywood vehicles offer us roles except as Suzy Wongs, Dragon Ladies, Charlie Chans, Fu Manchus, or docile domestic workers.

For people of color, ethnic groups, women, lesbians and gay men, and the disabled, the movie industry offers unrealistic portrayals and slanderous stereotypes. And audiences are influenced by what they see. The question becomes: how high a price must we pay to act in films?

Year of the Dragon is a typical racist, sexist Hollywood film. A white cop goes to New York City's Chinatown to clean up crime which is dominated by the "Chinese mafia" (the "tongs"). This glamorized urban Rambo falls for a Chinese American television reporter who epitomizes the exotic and submissive stereotype of Asian/Pacific American women.

I accepted a part as an extra in *Dragon* because it was an opportunity to act in a major production by a well-known director, Michael Cimino, and producer Dino De Laurentiis. Auditioning was exciting. I was proud to have worked my way up from casting directors to Cimino himself. Opportunities like this are few and far between—especially for Asian Americans actors. I worked 12-hour days, for meager pay ($50 a day). Smoke-machine fumes stifled the disco scene I appeared in. I could stand all that. There was even hope that my scene wouldn't end up on the cutting room floor!

Reading between the lines

I never saw the script of *Dragon*. But I had an idea about its premise and recalled some talk about it in the Asian American community.

While waiting to see if I'd gotten a part, I seriously weighed the pros and cons of acting in it.

The book behind the film (written by Robert Daley, who also wrote *Prince of the City*) turned out to be racist and sexist. I called contacts in the Asian American film and theater community in New York and the Bay Area for information and opinions about the film. Responses ranged from "Go for it—it's an opportunity for experience—you can put it on your résumé" to "It's a racist book—it'll be a racist film—protests against it may be organized when it's released."

An old friend, who plays one of the two redeeming Asian American characters in *Dragon*, said attempts were being made by some actors to effect changes from within, such as changing the content of the Cantonese dialogue to something realistic.

Generally speaking, however, actors have very little power over a film's content. The director, producer, and studio heads call the shots.

The dream shattered

When I decided to take the part as an extra, I also decided to participate in any protest organized against the film if it turned out to be reactionary.

At the press screening, my excitement about being in the movie turned quickly to anger—*Dragon* was far worse than I had ever expected. I felt used and exploited. The film was such a slap in the face to Chinese Americans and women—and Blacks, Puerto Ricans, Italians, Poles, the Irish...

After the screening, members of the National Asian American Telecommunications Association, in concert with other Chinatown community organizations and activists, called a meeting. I joined with others to form the Coalition Against *Year of the Dragon.*

The coalition linked itself to past organizing efforts against *Fort Apache,* which had slandered Puerto Ricans, and the obnoxious Charlie Chan film that sparked a boycott. The *Dragon* coalition gathered support for its exposé of the movie's bigotry. Even film critics understood the movie's reactionary message. They panned it and publicized a national boycott organized by coalitions in New York, Los Angeles, San Francisco,

Carolyn Brooks/*Freedom Socialist*

Seattle and Boston.

The protest succeeded. Box-office sales dropped. Threatened by losses, *Dragon's* distributors negotiated with the coalition. They wouldn't withdraw the film, but agreed to some superficial changes, such as adding a disclaimer that *Dragon* was not intended to be representative of real life in Chinatown.

Dual roles for actors

Television and news reporters were fascinated that, as an actor, I condemned the movie. Along with others, I used my connection with the film as a platform to publicize the boycott and educate about the dilemma facing Asian American actors.

Judging by the box-office failure of *Dragon,* Hollywood filmmakers have been sent a clear message that racism and sexism aren't marketable, and that the community is ready to boycott and protest exploitative films. Our protests showed the potential of the Asian American community and its allies to make Hollywood respect and reflect multicultural diversity.

As an actor, I see that my leading role is to work with others to reshape society's image of us and to express who we really are.

Legislating language:
Behind the attack on bilingualism
1986

by Pat Hirose

I first heard about the U.S. English movement in Bay
Area Latino and Asian community newspapers.
Activists and politicians quoted in these papers
denounced it. I didn't take it seriously, thinking that any
movement to legislate English as the official language of
California was merely an absurdity. Are the languages and
cultures of the non-English-speaking peoples—Chinese,
Japanese, Filipino, East Indian, Mexicano—who built
California's agriculture and industry undesirable, negli-
gible, something to be swept away by law?

As I said, I couldn't believe that the U.S. English movement was really serious. Then an "English as the Official
Language" initiative—Proposition 63—made it onto the
ballot for the upcoming November state elections.

I called the Mexican American Legal Defense Fund
(MALDEF) for more information about this initiative and
learned some brutal facts.

Proposition 63 proposes an amendment to the
California state constitution which would require state
officials to "take all steps necessary to insure that the role
of English as the common language of California is
enhanced." Anyone who resides or does business in
California could sue to enforce this measure.

In other words, all languages other than English
spoken by California residents will be relegated to official

nonexistence if the initiative passes.

Many essential life-support services for non-English-speaking people will be eliminated in short order. These include 911 telephone assistance, hospital and social service assistance, court interpreters, bilingual ballots, and bilingual education. The initiative would also clear the way for elimination of aid to language assistance programs for Latinos and Asians.

Any taxpayer could sue California's public libraries for subscribing to foreign language newspapers. Already, proponents of the initiative have asked the Federal Communications Commission to stop issuing licenses to foreign language radio stations in some areas of the state.

Behind the rhetoric

The U.S. English movement sponsoring this initiative, and similar ones across the country, is racist and xenophobic to the core.

The watchword of the movement is the need to preserve the national "identity"—the white Anglo-Saxon identity so beloved by the patriots. But this great "melting pot" ideal, which has historically justified racism under the guise of patriotism and been used to denigrate national cultures, is nothing but a justification for special exploitation and mistreatment of dark-skinned peoples, immigrants and U.S. nationals alike.

In effacing the cultural identity of the non-English-speaking and in blocking them from access to social services and full participation in society, the U.S. English honchos hope to maintain a vulnerable, docile, easily manipulated and politically impotent pool of super-exploitable labor for U.S. agriculture and industry.

Nothing illustrates the political intent of the U.S. English movement with more force and clarity than the campaign against bilingual education spearheaded by movement leader S.I. Hayakawa, the ultraconservative teacher and politician.

Bilingual education allows non-English-speaking students to maintain their own culture and language while making the transition into the mainstream language. Students are given instruction and information in their own tongue while learning English. This ensures a firmer grasp of the information needed to learn the second language properly.

Instruction in English only cuts off non-English-speaking students from their mother tongue and, in doing so, retards their ability to assimilate the second language.

The effect of lack of access to bilingual education on the non-English-speaking—on their ability to process needed information, to compete for jobs, to maintain their social organization, to defend themselves against oppression and exploitation—is devastating.

A spreading disease

Hayakawa and his ilk have garnered wide national support for their movement. Illinois, Indiana, Nebraska, Kentucky, Virginia, and Georgia have already adopted amendments similar to the one proposed in California.

Mexican American Legal Defense Fund attorneys are currently working at the federal level to prevent attachment of such an amendment to the Simpson-Rodino anti-immigration bill.

Florida, like California, will vote on the issue come November. Dade County adopted an English-only initiative several years ago. But, because of the large Cuban population, implementation of English-only services created so much chaos that some agencies reinstated bilingual services. The Cuban community there is mobilizing to repeal the initiative.

Protect our precious diversity

It is wholly unnecessary to legislate English as the official, exclusive U.S. language. English is overwhelmingly predominant in practice, and immigrants will learn it *of their own accord* in order to function in the U.S.

But the English-only movement is a cruel attempt to *forcibly* assimilate non-English-speaking immigrants into, and imprison them within, the lowest social and economic rungs of U.S. society. And as an attack on "foreign-ness"—specifically the cultures of immigrants of color—the campaign helps feed the general resurgence of racist rightwing jingoism being used as a club against all human rights in the "land of the free."

English-speaking and non-English-speaking people of color, workers, women, lesbians and gay men, and everyone else who feels the breath of rightwing reaction on their backs can and must organize now to protect the cultural and linguistic diversity that enriches this nation.

She's Gotta Have It:
A comedy in error

1987

by Cora Harris

She's Gotta Have It is a film which purports to turn the tables on the sex role game through a look at the life of a woman juggling relationships with three men. Independent filmmaker Spike Lee wrote, directed, edited, and starred in this movie, which features an all-Black cast.

The woman in question is Nola Darling. She is a graphic artist, although we never see her place of work. Instead, she is seen in her apartment, pasting up newspaper clippings of stories of police brutality and the murders of Black youths in a collage made to commemorate the birthday of Malcolm X. The subjects/themes of her art are the only references to Nola's political awareness or consciousness outside her sex life.

Other clues to her character are shown solely in the context of her relationship with the three men. She repeatedly tells us that she doesn't want to be owned by any man. This is the only thing she has to say for herself; at other times she is depressed or confused.

The men pursuing Nola are Greer Childs, an egotistical model/actor with pretensions to upperclass refinement; Jamie Overstreet, a romantic, conventional man who wants to make Nola his wife; and Mars Blackmon, an unemployed, sneaker-shod aficionado of rap music.

Contrary to Lee's stated intent to counter Hollywood's

depiction of Black men, all three are caricatures. The worst is Mars (played by Lee himself). Using the tired lowerclass stereotype, Lee portrays Mars as a hopeless, childlike buffoon.

Toward the end of the film, Jamie rapes Nola. This is a shocking, disturbing scene—and not just because rape is out of place in a comedy. Jamie is supposed to be mature and gentle, and is the only one Nola considers as a possible permanent lover. Prior to the rape, he and Nola have cooled their relationship because she has refused to choose among her lovers. She becomes despondent, invites Jamie to her apartment, and attempts to seduce him. Incensed at being "used" this way, he assaults her.

Jamie's *possessiveness* is the reason for his anger and the real motivation behind the rape. But this is obscured, and the audience is left with the impression that **Though ostensibly poking fun at possessive male attitudes, in reality the film reinforces the double standard.** Jamie is justified. Nola had "asked for it"—the old excuse for rape.

In a *New York Times* interview on August 10, 1986, Spike Lee said, "I think it's a very even look at relationships between Black men and women. The difference between this film and *The Color Purple* is that even though there are some dog men in this film, you can tell there is a difference. This film was not done with hate, and none of the men here are one-note animals like Mister was in *The Color Purple*."

It is hard to see how Greer, Jamie, and Mars are any better. Also, it is interesting that Lee felt the need to comment—in such a negative way—about a *Black feminist's* portrayal of Black men. Criticism of men by women is all too often equated to hatred of the gender. Yet Lee seems to feel that the depiction of Nola as a bewildered, vapid sex object is "even" and O.K.

Nor do the other women in the film do much for cinematic renditions of Black women. Nola seems to have only two female friends, one a former roommate and the other a lesbian named Opal Gilstrap. In one disappointing scene, Opal goes to comfort Nola and in the process makes a pass at her. Was it really necessary to dredge up yet another stereotype, that of the predatory dyke?

Also, with the exception of her roommate and Opal, Nola seems separate from other women. From her therapist, who does nothing to help her, to the women in her nightmares, other women are Nola's enemies—not allies.

Ostensibly, the film's purpose is to poke fun at the possessive, predictable attitudes of men, yet it *reinforces* the double standard. Lee focuses on Nola's sex life to the exclusion of everything else, and in the end she is less an independent woman than the "freak" everyone perceives her to be. In Spike Lee's own words, Nola is "acting like a man"—a pseudo male. And in thus stepping outside "women's role," Nola is fair game for depression, nightmares, and rape.

She's Gotta Have It is supposed to be a comedy, and there are some genuinely funny scenes. But on the whole, the laughter generated here leaves a bitter taste.

Harry Edwards' band-aid solutions: Sports and racism

1988

by Nancy Reiko Kato

Until recently, U.S. professional and college athletics have been run, practically unchallenged, as blatantly racist plantation systems. White professional team owners and college administrators are the plantation masters.

They make big dollars off the athletes, the majority of whom are Black.

Last year, baseball executive Al Campanis of the Los Angeles Dodgers stated that Blacks "may not have some of the necessities" to become big league managers. Outrage exploded nationwide against racism in U.S. sports. The Dodgers summarily fired Campanis, not out of concern for racial equality, but from fear of public scrutiny and condemnation of the plantation.

The Al Campanises and Jimmy the Greeks have made these kinds of comments for years without provoking much ado. But now, after racist attacks on people of color in Howard Beach and Forsyth County, resurgent Black anger and activism have turned the heat up under the racists.

Good business

In an attempt to defuse protest over the absence of Blacks in top coaching and executive positions, major league baseball commissioner Peter Ueberroth hired

Black sports activist Harry Edwards to develop an affirmative action plan for baseball. Edwards, a sociology professor at the University of California at Berkeley, was the first to characterize sports as a plantation system, and his perceptions of the factors that perpetuate **Athletics mirror prevailing institutions and attitudes and will change when these conditions are uprooted.**
sports racism are acute. But his solutions to the problem are band-aid measures at best.

Edwards wants to *reform* the system, i.e., keep it intact, but "correct" the injustices. He proposes to convince professional owners that it's in their self-interest to promote Black equality, if only to ensure greater player loyalty to the leagues.

Pro owners will likely make some cosmetic changes. But equality? The bosses' self-interest starts and stops with profits, and profits are the flip side of discrimination.

Racism has been especially good to the sports moguls. Lack of equal opportunity elsewhere for Blacks has provided the owners with a captive pool of aspiring Black athletes. Race hatred also helped bust the Black-led National Football League players' strike last fall: union head Gene Upshaw got plenty of racist hate mail during and after the strike, as did at least one player rep, Seattle's Kenny Easley.

Does Edwards really think that the owners are going to break up the skin game that serves them so well?

Boycott

The boycott remains Edwards' weapon of "last resort" against collegiate injustice. Meanwhile, he advises Black high school athletes to reject those universities that deny equal access to top coaching and administrative positions for Blacks.

How would such an approach, by itself, win lasting and fundamental change?

Even if schools were to open up their coaching and administrative ranks, what good would it do if the social and economic conditions that perpetuate inequality remain? Businesses hire people of color and women these days as turncoat overseers to better control discriminatory workplaces. How would it be any different in collegiate sports, where the money comes largely from exploiting and discarding poor Black youngsters?

Eyes on the prize

Athletic reforms *are* necessary, to alleviate exploitation and as a bridge to winning control of the game by athletes and fans.

Boycotts, targeting high-profile universities and linking up with other campus struggles—free speech and anti-apartheid struggles, for example—could send shock waves throughout the university system. And they would stand a greater chance of success if they were to demand equal access for other people of color and women along with Blacks.

Other demands would include a plan guaranteeing that colleges provide athletes with a sound education and training for life outside sports. Profits from games should be put into educational resources and student services such as tutoring, counseling, health care, and ethnic, labor, and women's studies that teach students their real history.

In both college and pro ranks, segregation by position, especially blatant in football, must be eliminated. No more reserving the "glamour" positions for whites. Let's have more Black and Latino quarterbacks. And why not Asian American linebackers, Indian running backs? There should be equal pay for all positions in the pros, because in team sports all positions are equally important.

The college draft system, an instrument for owner

control which sells athletes off like livestock, should be abolished. Players, like all workers, should be able to choose whom they want to work for. Their right to unionize must be recognized as absolute. And players and coaches should share in revenue gained from television, tickets, and advertisements.

The push for reforms can begin to attack the racism and inequality in sports. But if we are to eliminate inequality, the push must connect to the larger struggles against race, sex, and class oppression in this country. Athletics mirror the prevailing institutions and attitudes that victimize people of color, women and the poor, and will change for good when these conditions are uprooted.

When that happens, society will truly be able to fulfill its athletic potential.

Huerta, brutal cops, and the UFW

1989

by Moisés Montoya

On September 14, 1988, the Tactical Squad of the San Francisco Police Department attacked demonstrators protesting a visit by President George Bush. They beat several demonstrators severely, including United Farm Workers Union Vice President Dolores Huerta, who suffered broken ribs and a ruptured spleen.

Such brutality is an increasingly typical police response to peaceful protests nationwide. Why? The economy is floundering: times are bad and getting worse. The government has walked out on the people. Little by little, everyone feels their safety net being yanked away: jobs, homes, health care, social security, education... People are angry and restless—and the police are there to keep "order."

It's not that people in power are blind to the growing misery. Rather, they understand that if people win demands for equality, a fair share, an end to the status quo, those now at the top are out of business. They pay the police, and buy politicians, to maintain things as they are.

Meanwhile, who is hardest hit by bad times? It's people of color, immigrants, lesbians and gay men, women, the working poor—those who are traditionally discriminated against and despised. They're also the ones hardest hit by police.

These groups are organizing and fighting back against

job loss and budget cuts, racism and gay-bashing and anti-abortion attacks. They're headed toward major collision with the system. This is why Dolores Huerta got beaten.

Some still think, despite the growing evidence, that the have-nots can achieve their demands with the aid of "friends" in the establishment, i.e., Democrats. But the poor have no buddies among the powers-that-be: they are on opposite sides of the line because their *interests* are completely opposed. The powerful never forget it, and the poor must never forget it either.

Sometimes, however, they do.

Soft-pedaling the issue

A case in point is the UFW's response to Huerta's beating. Following the atrocity, a well-attended meeting was held in San Francisco's largely Latino Mission District to deal with the community's shock and anger. Most people wanted to denounce the outrage and organize against police brutality. But the chair, San Francisco Supervisor Jim Gonzalez, and the UFW representative, Howard Wallace, worked to steer the crowd away from the issue and toward discussion of the UFW's grape boycott.

Gonzalez did promise to investigate "police misconduct"—but later *defended* police at a public hearing!

The message to the police: go and sin again.

The UFW leadership has long oriented toward pacifism, reformism, and friendly relations with the Democratic Party. And they did not want to speak out against the police because this might threaten their courtship of liberal city officials and assorted labor bureaucrats. In the September issue of their magazine, *Food and Justice,* they even claimed that Huerta was not involved in the demo at which she was beaten!

The UFW has fought hard over the years and won many victories for farmworkers. And the grape boycott deserves enthusiastic support. But it is self-defeating and ultimately impossible to completely separate the boycott from police brutality and related issues that degrade and destroy the people that the UFW wishes to defend!

Toning down protest so as not to offend Democrats merely impedes the UFW's work. All the smiles in Sacramento and Washington, D.C. haven't kept farmworkers from dying of pesticide poisoning or gained for them a decent life.

That work awaits completion. We can speed it along by making San Francisco police accountable for what they did to Dolores Huerta and by demanding a Civilian Review Board, composed of elected community representatives, that will step in against further brutalities.

We urge the UFW to join in this work and in constructing a multi-issue coalition that will work effectively to end police abuse *and* build the grape boycott. What better way to bring farmworkers and other cop victims together?

The cops and the Democrats won't like it. What better recommendation is there than that?

¡Basta con la chota!
¡Que viva la huelga!

Mississippi Burning:
A celluloid sellout

1989

by Yolanda Alaniz

I sat in the theater, stunned and incredulous. Watching the movie *Mississippi Burning,* I found myself burning up at this sickening caricature of the 1960s civil rights movement.

The film is based on an actual event, the racist murders of three brave young activists—Mickey Schwerner, James Chaney and Andy Goodman—in Philadelphia, Mississippi. But the movie rewrites history. The real heroes of the Freedom Summer of 1964 were these youths and their comrades. The heroes of *Mississippi Burning* are the white FBI agents who come to town looking for their bodies.

The film accurately shows that the governor, mayor, sheriff and local police, all members or sympathizers of the Ku Klux Klan, conspired to murder the civil rights workers and hide their bodies, and that the silence of the white community gave them the green light.

Organized racist terror is powerfully portrayed. But the casting of Blacks as minor characters and passive victims, who are only saved by the intervention of noble emissaries of the "great white father" in Washington, D.C., is a vicious and bigoted lie. Not only does such a premise ignore the prolonged, intransigent mass movement which alone changed Mississippi—and the rest of the South—permanently. It completely falsifies the role of the feds, which was always a major part of the problem.

In the picture, Gene Hackman and Willem Dafoe star as sensitive federal agents who serve justice. In life, the federal government was only dragged into the case by a tremendous public outcry. The FBI finally responded with a ludicrous media event, in which hundreds of white agents and sailors converged on the town searching for the bodies. The theater audience laughed, but it really happened.

The movie fashions a triumphant ending out of the discovery of the bodies and the convictions won on charges of violating the victims' civil rights. It leaves out the vile true conclusion—none of the assassins who were sentenced served more than five years of jail time.

The state of Mississippi was not about to bring criminal charges against the killers. To bring the southern police states to heel, the U.S. government would have had to launch a new Reconstruction, as was done after the Civil War. This would have had revolutionary consequences North *and* South. So the federal charges of civil rights violations under the Fourteenth Amendment were Washington's wholly inadequate substitute for justice.

Method behind the amnesia

As I left the theater, I asked myself, why produce such a warped picture? And why now?

Hollywood could have inspired and educated a generation born after the civil rights movement and untutored in this proud chapter of U.S.—and world—history. Instead, the propagandists packaged a sanitized image of the FBI as friend and savior of social movements.

FBI and other government agents in the '60s were openly hostile, infiltrating and destabilizing organizations, orchestrating acts of terrorism in order to justify witch hunts. They wanted to discredit Dr. Martin Luther King, Jr., even hoping to drive him to suicide, by spreading rumors that he was a communist and adulterer.

Today, they are often more sophisticated. They pose as good guys, advising the naive to trust the government, adopt nonviolence as a *principle,* and avoid direct confrontation with Nazis and rightwing anti-abortionists. They use their influence with liberals to persuade the movement to tie its own hands.

The makers of *Mississippi Burning* got the message, and they're delivering it to us. Obediently, they show us that faith in the federal government, not mass action, produces social and political change.

Truth and consequences

History will not be rewritten so easily. The civil rights struggle accomplished a world of change for all of us, no matter what our color or sex. The movement's true story is told in works like *Three Lives for Mississippi,* William Bradford Huie's account of the Philadelphia murders.

Reading Huie's book, I was struck by the dedication of Schwerner, Goodman, and Chaney. They were three martyrs, two Jewish and one Black, among thousands of Black and white women and men who were the backbone of the civil rights movement, building such organizations as SNCC (Student Nonviolent Coordinating Committee), CORE (Congress of Racial Equality), and COFO (Council of Federated Organizations).

The time will come soon when such spirited youth will rise again to fulfill the potential of the civil rights movement. We have not yet gained either economic equality or full democratic rights, which will only come with workers' control of society. In a system ruled by profits, the reemergence of KKK and fascist ambitions is inevitable.

Building a new, revolutionary Freedom Now movement is the way to make sure that Schwerner, Chaney, Goodman and the hundreds of others who were beaten, killed, or lynched did not fight in vain.

We remember the real truth of their fight. And we will carry it on!

Huey Newton, 1942-1989:
Tribute to a fallen warrior
1990

by Tom Boot

A hot August sun bore down on the quiet, pensive crowd gathered outside Allen Temple Baptist Church in East Oakland, California.

Hundreds of people—anxious, disciplined, young and old, a mostly Black though integrated crowd from the neighborhood and surrounding community—assembled to pay tribute to brother and revolutionary Huey P. Newton.

I was caught up in the charged silence. Images, memories and conclusions swirled through my mind.

A similar scene almost 25 years earlier: Faith Temple, 147th Street and Amsterdam in Harlem, February 1965, the funeral of Malcolm X. What does it mean for Black people to have their radical leadership continually murdered or bought off?

Allen Temple and its vestibules were filled to overflow capacity. Those of us outside were separated from the service inside by an ominous gate. Here, a necessary separation, but one that brought reflections of past and present unnatural separations: Jim Crow. Segregation. The ghetto.

Loudspeakers amplified the service. Militant words from Bobby Seale, Erika Huggins, Johnny Spain and Elaine Brown entered ears and activated minds. Until, mysteriously, a major underground cable connecting the outside with the service inside was severed. Was somebody afraid of us that day? Afraid that the words would not only activate minds but a new movement?

Competitive national media crews climbed the church roof for photos and footage. Would they show reality? Would the statement of Reverend Pinkard be broadcast? "They called Huey P. Newton a gangster. But we know who the gangsters are."

Huey Newton was not made into a legend or folk hero that day. There were no mythologizing eulogies.

Rather his story was simply retold. Immortalized were Huey's unique contributions and commitment to this terribly long struggle for Black freedom. His radical, investigative genius, his concern for the people, his desire for revolutionary change were extolled.

> By surrendering my life to revolution,
> I found eternal life,
> Revolutionary Suicide.
>
> — Huey P. Newton,
> "Revolutionary Suicide"

Newton organized the Panthers' armed and defiant demonstration on the capitol steps of Sacramento in 1967. The revolutionary fire from this action ignited the spirit, hopes and actions of Black people.

The white racist power structure was paralyzed—momentarily. And liberal, pacifist Black leadership stood aside, aghast.

By this single act, the Panthers grabbed the horns of a dilemma—the question of reform or revolution—still being endlessly debated today. The Panthers quite logically deduced and codified the answer: Black liberation necessitated revolutionary change.

Many of us agreed with "We Believe," the Panthers' 10-point program, a bold indictment of the U.S. government, which called for the overthrow of capitalism.

Panthers were community activists. They established children's breakfast programs, free schools and medical clinics.

Critically important was the denunciation by Newton and the Panthers of Black cultural nationalism and separatism. Dashikis might be vogue and Mother Africa's roots consoling, but practically speaking, that is the extent of it. Moreover, cultural nationalist bromides concealed the insidious message that Black capitalists are the saviors of the race. But what of Black workers, sweated by bosses of all colors? The problem was the *system,* and to destroy it the Panthers sought unity among all oppressed races.

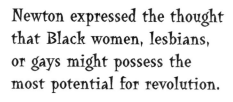 **Newton expressed the thought that Black women, lesbians, or gays might possess the most potential for revolution.**

Newton defended Black women's equality, condemned homophobia, and sharpened the cutting edge of our consciousness. He expressed the thought that perhaps the Black woman, lesbian, or gay, as the most vilified of the community, possesses the most potential for rebellion. The Panthers' condemnation of nationalism and sexism remains critically important for me, a light-skinned Black gay radical, and for us all.

Speeches, tributes and eulogies quickly fade from memory, as do the specifics of that August memorial.

However, Huey's revolutionary spirit will remain.

No COINTELPRO-style massacres, no government rampages can stomp out the meaning behind the slogan "Free Huey," now synonymous with "Free the People."

It has been said that the movement in the '60s was about plowing new ground and any movement now is about protecting old ground.

But while protecting the old ground being rapidly torn apart by racist reaction, we must move quickly to do more. Critical problems affecting Black people are far worse than 20 years ago: poverty, unemployment, homelessness, police brutality, drugs, George Bush's genocidal "anti-drug" war.

What does it mean for Black people to have their radical leadership continually wiped out? With Huey, Malcolm X and others gone, we need new leaders, a revolutionary program and decisive action now.

As former Panther Geronimo ji Jaga (Pratt) said, we must "take Huey's spirit and use it to enhance our struggle and forever move forward."

Black or African American— what's in a name?

1990

by Tom Boot

O vernight, the term African American has become the current touted nomenclature within large segments of the Black community and press. The transition occurred so swiftly that it seemed my usual Black self went to sleep one night and awoke the following morning greeted by a chorus of "Good morning, Mr. African American!" My response? I don't like it!

Go ahead, say it's an identity crisis. Worse yet, label me one of those Booker T. Washington-type Negroes. Regardless, I sense something politically askew here.

I realize that African American is used interchangeably with Black or Black American. But more and more it's being used to the exclusion of the latter. (The more nationalist, professionally affluent, or politically mainstream the sector of the community, the more the tendency to use African American.) But just the fact that so many, from Jesse Jackson and Supreme Court Justice Thurgood Marshall to the *New Amsterdam News,* are using the term doesn't make it right.

What's in a name?

This isn't the first name change that Black people in America have gone through. There have been several through the centuries, each motivated by politics.

I grew up in an era when we called ourselves Negroes

and were proud of it.

Then, as a result of that awesome combustion of the civil rights movement, we rightfully titled ourselves Afro-Americans. To call oneself Afro-American was to reject the "nigger" status that had come to be associated with the term "Negro" and to bathe in a multitude of new discoveries— those myriad rivers of cul- **Our Blackness expresses the militant contour, purpose, direction, and resolve of our struggle against racism.** tural expression and identity flooding the times.

But other changes were in store. The term Black American was born at the apex of the Black Power movement. Intense political and physical confrontation with the Kennedy/Johnson regimes and racist reactionaries around the country left us with no recourse but to stand defiant and demand our personhood as Blacks and Americans.

"Blackness" denoted a militant racial identity and affirmed the worth of those who had been exploited, persecuted, segregated, and discriminated against because of the color of our skin. "Black" made positive what had for so long been negative in racist America.

The term signaled a political transformation in us—our unwillingness to accept second-class status, our demand for radical change in a country that profited off the degradation of an "inferior" race. Not surprisingly, it took Black conservatives, the press, and mainstream America a long time to come to terms with the name change.

Sleight of hand

Now on our doorstep, suddenly, and after a decade of Reaganite reaction, comes another transformation of nomenclature. We're no longer Blacks, but African Americans. Why?

I think some, not all, of those putting forward the new term consciously or unconsciously want to turn away from the real problems Black Americans face today, problems that are, as ever, rooted in racism. Yes, racism still exists in the good old U.S. of A.

I am not so concerned with our Africanness as with our Blackness, which expresses the militant contour, purpose, direction and resolve of our struggle to overcome racism. And it is this struggle which I think Jesse Jackson and others who promote the term African American are trying to obscure. After all, it's very difficult to deal with what capitalism does every day to Black people here in the U.S.

It's as if—after a decade of hearing both Reaganites and liberals claim that racism no longer exists, that the laws make everybody "equal" now, hence that any problems Blacks still have are our own fault—the assertion of racial identity and worth is somehow an act of bad manners, or an attitude problem.

It's as if in calling ourselves African Americans we can assume equality with whites—Irish Americans, Italian Americans, other ethnic groups. It's as if we can bring an end to the pain through a languid, indulgent identification with a long ago past.

But what of the present, racist reality?

Genuine roots

To find pride in one's historic roots and cultural identity can be meritorious and rewarding, but not if it involves exclusion of our present reality. Let's not forget that most Black Americans are centuries removed from any direct link to Africa.

Unlike many ethnic groups in America who are only several generations removed from European, Asian or Latin American heritage, Black Americans represent a culture that, though some of its elements were born in Africa, has been shaped and created on American soil, under conditions of racial exclusion. We must be accorded the rights and recognition that we have earned through our blood, sweat and tears—as Black Americans.

Our strongest link to Africa today lies in our solidarity with various African peoples fighting for their liberation. And while our ties are strengthened by physical/genetic commonalities, we need to get on with the job of liberating ourselves here in America, even as we demand freedom for our South African sisters and brothers.

Liberation means fighting against racism here and now, just as it did in the '60s, when we became Black.

Betting is hardly a scientific, let alone reputable, venture for a Marxist. But what the heck—I bet you that we will witness the term African American ride a short-lived bout of popularity and then disappear in direct relation to the impending upsurge in our Black liberation struggle.

Miss Saigon:
Money calls a racist tune
1991

by Nellie Wong

O ne would think, as we advance into the last decade of the 20th century, that multicultural reality would dictate the right of people of color—Chinese, Blacks, Vietnamese, Latinos/Chicanos, Native Americans, any racial group to which one belongs—to portray ourselves on stage and screen.

Not so, as shown by the controversy raging since mid-1990 over the casting of *Miss Saigon,* a musical play due to hit Broadway this spring.

Miss Saigon, an update of *Madame Butterfly,* is set in Vietnam in 1975, as U.S. forces are withdrawing in defeat. Jonathan Pryce, a white actor who plays the Eurasian male lead in the London production, is producer Cameron Mackintosh's choice to play the role in New York. The Asian American and other communities of color have loudly denounced the choice.

Actors' Equity, bowing to protest, first barred Pryce from taking the role.

Mackintosh then canceled the Broadway run, after ringing up $25 million in advance sales, to force a reversal by Equity. The union caved in. *Miss Saigon* will come to Broadway. Pryce will play the lead.

Money talks

Asian American actors wanted the right to be auditioned for the lead, but were never given the opportunity. No one is brazen enough to say that there aren't any qualified Asian actors, but that is still the underlying racist assumption.

Supposedly, there aren't any "bankable" Asian American actors who can "carry" the play. It's believed no one would want to see an Asian American starring, at least no one who can afford a $100 ticket to *Miss Saigon*.

Once again, money considerations are used as a rationale for injustice. And lurking behind the rationale is, again, the idea that somehow an Asian actor can't act well enough or isn't "charismatic" enough to draw the crowds.

You'd think that the recent success of the movie *Dances with Wolves*—whose Native American actors are acclaimed as essential to the picture's realism, emotional wallop, and drawing power—would have changed some minds on this score.

Nonetheless, in the megabucks-dominated American theater, the Cameron Mackintoshes will likely continue to place "bankable" white actors in all the leading roles, and to hell with equal opportunity.

Spurious reasoning

Asian American actors and playwrights and their allies—other actors of color and community activists—have protested the dearth of opportunity in the casting of *Miss Saigon* and achieved some results. The "yellow face" makeup worn in the London production has disappeared.

This being so, Cameron had to scramble to justify using Pryce in the role. Though Asian Americans who have read the libretto say the role calls for a Vietnamese, Mackintosh defined the character as half French—hence the European Pryce can play him with as little affront to justice as an Asian could. It's six one way, half dozen the other, right?

Sure, as soon as Eurasians in this society are no longer discriminated against—as people of color.

So long as Mackintosh's bogus thinking rules in mainstream theater, Asian American actors will continue to play only the kind of supporting roles—houseboys, cooks, etc.—that have traditionally been theirs. They should be grateful they're onstage at all; that is the message that the power brokers of the theater industry are sending.

For multicultural equality

Plays produced by Asian American theater companies in San Francisco, Los Angeles, Seattle, and New York City can obviously fulfill only part of the need for Asian Americans to play ourselves.

Those Asian American actors with roles in *Miss Saigon* should push to open up opportunities for their brother and sister actors of color, in starring roles and character parts as well. Actors' Equity must support them. And the public should boycott the show. That means enlisting support from labor and other movements.

In this stacked system, we have to organize from within and without to make change. That's what the Black civil rights movement did in the '60s and early '70s. And while Black actors are a long way from having won equality, you can bet that Hollywood and Broadway wouldn't dare put a white actor in a Black role today. The movement would crucify any producer who tried such a stunt.

In a multicultural America that denies equality, I'm not fooled by a few faces of color appearing in magazines and on the stage, screen, TV, and billboards. Money still rules the arts and media. And the long green dictates that a disproportionate number of faces we see there are white.

When creative freedom is no longer stifled by the almighty dollar, then we'll see the flourishing of real multiculturalism: yellows, blacks, browns, reds, and whites—women and men, lesbian and gay and straight—looming as large in theaters and on movie screens as we are in life.

Blacks and Asians:
We are NOT enemies

1991

by Darryl Powell and Emily Woo Yamasaki

N ew York City media barons decided they'd struck
pay dirt last year with the chance to sensationalize
the Black community boycott of two Korean
markets in Flatbush.

Tabloid headlines flashed when the boycott was
triggered by a Haitian woman's charge that a Korean
shopkeeper had unjustly accused her of shoplifting and
then assaulted her.

Both the media and the city fathers figured the controversy would serve as a handy counterweight to the uproar
over white racism in the murders of Black men in Howard
Beach and Bensonhurst. See, screamed the nightly news
broadcasts, Blacks and Asians are racist too!

But the picketers and boycott organizers we've talked
to are not anti-Asian bigots. They point to good relations
between some Korean store owners and the predominantly Black communities they serve. But the two stores in
question are notorious for their disdainful treatment of the
people in their communities, and for that reason we
believe this boycott was justified.

Divide and conquer

The city's actions reinforce our belief: the press called
the boycott organizers "outside agitators," when in fact
they were community people, primarily Haitians. Then,

New York's first Black mayor, David Dinkins, crossed the picket line to buy fruit. And the police, for whom Black community self-organizing is anathema, used the boycott to harass picketers and clamp down on street vendors.

Little wonder that, after the Korean shopkeeper was acquitted in January 1991 of assault on the Haitian woman, some Blacks have concluded that the system works for Asians but not for them.

The city fathers played their old divide-and-conquer game. But the truth of this situation is that the system doesn't work for *anyone*—except the rich.

Bombarded by stereotypes

As an Asian American woman and an African American man, we are keenly aware that our communities have sometimes been in conflict, and not just in New York. In recent years, incidents of mistrust, race-baiting and violence have erupted between U.S. or Caribbean Blacks and Koreans, Vietnamese, and other Asian and Pacific Islander groups from L.A. to Boston.

Why? Are our cultures so incompatible that we inevitably clash? Are people natural racists and xenophobes?

We don't believe it.

We do believe that this system invests a lot of energy in *teaching* racism. We're bombarded with, and sometimes buy into, the hype: Asian immigrants are the "model minority" that steals jobs from American workers; Blacks, meanwhile, are lazy, would rather be on welfare than hold jobs, are natural thieves, ad nauseam.

These are the stereotypes. What's behind them? And who benefits?

Racist politics equals capitalist economics

We find the answer to the above questions in the fact that while oppressed people are at each others' throats, white male bosses and landlords get rich off a discriminatory wage system and exorbitant rents for slum housing.

That's the capitalist stake in keeping us divided. If we're tied up fighting each other, we won't be struggling together against the real enemy.

And as economic recession deepens, Blacks, Koreans, and all the oppressed will be pushed toward more frantic squabbling over dwindling jobs, housing, financing for homes and small businesses, and other pieces of the shrinking economic pie. The powers-that-be are hoping we'll think that our own group's survival hinges on another's demise.

That's why cultural nationalism—which sees race, not class, as the primary dividing line among us—isn't the answer. Poor Blacks and Koreans struggling to make it *aren't* each others' enemies. The system which serves the money-men who are pitting us against one another is the problem.

Marcel Hatch

And that is a problem that won't be solved by "Buy Black" campaigns, either. Control of all wealth is in white capitalist hands. And even if we could do business entirely within our own community, we would still be stuck in an economic ghetto, with a few of our own added to the ranks of the exploiters.

We need to unite

Rather than scapegoat each other, we need to build multiracial *alliances*—based on respect and recognition of the real economic and social walls that divide us.

And we can do it. Last year in Tacoma, Washington, a group including Korean Americans, Blacks, other people of color, whites, and radicals rallied together outside a pro-Nazi Populist Party meeting. Demonstrators were protesting Populist links to an Aryan Nations plot to bomb Korean businesses, a Black nightclub, a gay disco, and Jewish synagogues. Those Nazis sure saw we had something in common. Fortunately, so did the anti-Populist protesters.

Obviously, it's urgent we get past our divisions. We should begin holding inter-community dialogues that educate about our diverse cultures and histories. The Flatbush boycott sparked vital discussions, including forums organized by Radical Women in New York and San Francisco. African American and Asian American feminists Barbara Smith and Merle Woo talked at these forums about both the difficulties and necessity of uniting across the color line, and most people in the racially diverse audiences agreed that we can only win by working together.

Racial antagonism among people of color is, like white racism and like sexism and anti-gay bigotry, a cornerstone of the capitalist system that sits on our backs. We have to break through that antagonism and get rid of that system. As that happens, racial and ethnic diversity will become the occasion not for hostility, but for celebration.

Campus wars over Ethnic Studies

1992

by Merle Woo

T hird World strikes swept U.S. campuses 22 years ago. Students, staff, faculty, and community activists shut down colleges and won Ethnic Studies, affirmative action, and educational opportunity programs.

Today, students who want to maintain those gains are pushing for the establishment of Ethnic Studies Requirements (ESR) that would oblige students to fulfill a certain number of credits by studying racism and people of color. With the growing number of racist attacks on campuses, it is students of color who realize what's at stake. If the bigot thugs are not stopped, no student of color will be safe; thus students of color will effectively be barred from higher education. So the need for education about race as a tool to curtail racist violence becomes an urgent task.

But college administrators and white conservative faculty are trying to block ESR. They accuse ESR proponents of trying to mandate "political correctness." And they charge that ESR will lower academic standards and censor free speech!

One strategy used against ESR is the substitution of a much broader American Pluralism Requirement (APR), which can be satisfied by taking courses about gender, racism, lesbians and gays, European immigration, or even Celtic literature. While APR covers some crucial areas of study, it dilutes ESR's much-needed emphasis on race.

"If it ain't white, it ain't right"

The argument that ESR violates free speech goes like this: For universities to require the study of people of color and their viewpoints is the same as *espousing* those viewpoints. And when students of color demand courses on contributions made by their people to U.S. economic and social life, they are stifling the free speech of white students and imposing a burdensome chore on the faculty.

The companion claim that ESR will erode academic standards is in itself racist. It's saying that learning about people of color and how they view themselves and the world is "lightweight"! The message is that when education is not white enough, not male enough, and not straight enough, it is worthless.

Besides that, says the white elite, what is taught in Ethnic Studies is wrong, rhetorical, and more than likely fabricated.

A Black faculty member and published scholar who teaches that Greek civilization flowered because of African influence is, according to the conserva- **The message is that when education is not white, male, or straight enough, it is worthless.**

tives, pushing a "political line"; therefore, his work is discounted. On the other hand, a white European male who teaches that only whites made Greece great is considered erudite, highly academic, and absolutely truthful.

And who gets to set the standards? That's right, the white male academics.

One is Dinesh D'Souza, author of *Illiberal Education* and the reactionaries' well-funded boy jouster against the "political correctness" dragon. He attacks affirmative action and warns that Mickey Mouse courses on Black, Chicano, American Indian, and Asian American literature threaten to replace "real" literature—that written by DWEM (dead white European men).

Truth will set you free

Why are these spokespersons for the dead so threatened by ESR and even APR? Some reasons come to mind:

What would happen in education if Native Americans taught that Columbus did not discover America but instead launched 500 years of racism, oppression, and land theft?

What would happen if African Americans taught the history of Black Reconstruction, when former slaves passed pioneering social legislation including public funding for schools and orphanages?

What would happen if Jews taught classes about the Holocaust and explained the role of big business in fascism's rise?

What if Chicanos and Asian Americans educated about their long history of militant labor organizing?

The truth is dangerous—at least to the oppressor. These kinds of classes would express not just a "supplemental" viewpoint, but one diametrically opposed to the status-quo political line of the ruling class—the one that taught us Columbus discovered America.

Opponents of Ethnic Studies Requirements, or even the existence of Ethnic Studies, don't want students to think critically or question the foundations of capitalism—racism, sexism, homophobia, national chauvinism, and class exploitation. The political awakening of students, especially students of color, is their worst nightmare.

The best defense is a united offense

As Malcolm X said, "Of all our studies, history is best qualified to reward our research." To win strong Ethnic Studies programs, students of color need only look at their own history and build on it. In the '60s, Ethnic Studies was achieved through Third World student strikes and united fronts. Oppressed students formed these united fronts by forging connections to the communities from which they came and by linking up with staff and faculty.

History also teaches what doesn't work—like relying on liberal faculty who will sell out for academic privileges. Students at the University of Washington in Seattle recently learned this the hard way. The students "compromised" with liberal academics who urged them to accept American Pluralism instead of an Ethnic Studies Requirement and to keep quiet. In the meantime, the conservatives counter-organized—and when the vote came up, liberals joined with the conservatives to vote the American Pluralism Requirement down. The students ended up with neither an Ethnic Studies Requirement nor an American Pluralism Requirement.

Nice, quiet ways have never won civil rights or student demands; they didn't stop the Vietnam War. They won't win an Ethnic Studies Requirement or even an American Pluralism Requirement. Let's all take a wake-up pill and realize that radical united action has once again got to be at the top of our agenda.

Jews on the Left:
Don't turn right!
1991

by Henry Noble

I wish to address my antiwar *landsmen,* my fellow Jews, now being pressured to forsake the Left and bow down before the U.S. and Israeli governments. Thousands of Jews marched in the many protests of Bush's Gulf war. We were in the streets before the January 17, 1991 onslaught and after, while hundreds of thousands of bombs rained on Iraq and occasional Iraqi Scuds fell on Tel Aviv. When a quarter-million people rallied against the war January 26 in Washington, D.C., more than 50,000 were Jews, according to the *Washington Post.* I was one of the many who participated in the antiwar movement in the other Washington.

But Jewish nationalists have equated opposing the war to being an enemy of Israel. And, according to their "logic," any enemy of Israel is an anti-Semite.

Big lie: anti-Zionism = anti-Semitism

Consider this letter from Jerusalem printed in the last *Freedom Socialist:* "I have just experienced a month of Scuds. Kindly *stop* sending me your anti-Semitic newspaper."

The *FS* isn't anti-Semitic. All my FSP comrades promote Jewish liberation and fight discrimination against Jews as vigorously as they fight all bigotry.

The letter writer falsely equates resistance to Zionism

with anti-Semitism.

Don't be fooled.

Zionism is a rightwing ideology based on an alleged "historical right" to an exclusively Jewish state in Palestine. It arose in the 1800s as a reaction to pogroms and discrimination, but remained a minority movement until the Jewish Holocaust. After World War II, the victorious nations embraced the Jewish state. Israel would serve two functions: it would be a dumping ground for the Jewish refugees spurned by Western countries, and it would be a breakwater against the rising tide of Arab revolution.

Revolutionary socialists like Leon Trotsky warned that a Zionist state would stand Jewish humanism on its head—negating a progressive tradition dating back thousands of years—and turn into a death trap for Jews.

They were right. Today, Israel is a militaristic, sexist, racist theocracy.

Because of the history of the Zionist state and its utter dependence on the West, it could not be otherwise. Its economy functions only through ceaseless infusions of massive foreign capital. It did not organically evolve; rather, it was created by the expulsion and suppression of the indigenous people, which spawned a resistance that makes this "haven" the most dangerous place on earth to be a Jew.

Many Israelis fight for democratic reforms, but these cannot be realized short of a *radical* transformation to a secular, multi-ethnic, socialist country freed from the necessity to serve as the military, political, and economic outpost of Western imperialism in the Middle East.

Opportunity beckoned

The strong public opposition to the Gulf war gave U.S. Jews a golden anvil. We could have used it to forge movement solidarity against divide-and-conquer tactics.

Jews could have taught that the Arab masses—not Western crusaders—will end the despotism of Saddam and the sheiks and emirs. We could have argued that lasting security for the region's Jews depends not on Israel's allegiance to imperialism, but on revolutionary unity between Arab masses and Jewish workers.

Who better than U.S. Jews to assert the need to include Palestinian demands in any peace agreement? Or to puncture the myth of Israeli "restraint" during the war by revealing Israel's role in intelligence-gathering and strategy-development?

Who better to condemn the anti-Arab racism that eventually infected the antiwar movement itself? Or to castigate the big media, which humanized American and Israeli casualties but censored the unthinkable Iraqi devastation and loss of life? Or to expose as humbug the comparison of Saddam and Hitler?

Some of us did so, when we could get to a mike. (Often those running the show tried to censor radical opinions.)

But some well-known Jewish activists on the *other side* found ample outlets for wooing Jewish support of the U.S. war on the false basis of protecting Israel. These cowards capitulated to the might of their own capitalists rather than stand up to the warmongering of the U.S. and Israel.

John Judis, social democrat and *In These Times* writer, defends Bush's war and smears the antiwar coalitions as anti-Semitic. He tells Jews to leave the Left or fight to purge it of both anti-Semitism (meaning anti-Zionism) and what he calls "excessive anti-Americanism."

Tikkun magazine editor Michael Lerner urges us to join with other patriots who are, in his words, proud of their country's "higher moral purpose" in the war to "contain Saddam."

Our fate is everyone's fate

Jews who felt genuinely ambivalent protesting the war while worrying about the safety of Holocaust survivors, refugees, and loved ones in Israel should know that there is a solution—but it requires rejection of the Zionist crap. Most know instinctively that you cannot base a safe and just society on the oppression of another people. But Jews have been conditioned to believe Israel is different. Believe me, it isn't. Ask a West Bank resident.

Saving Jews is important. Saving Iraqis, Kurds, Moslems and Palestinians is important. Who can know whose child will grow up to cure cancer or AIDS?

Jews must stay in the Left to further their proud history of struggle and advocacy for the oppressed and to insure that socialism achieves its internationalist, democratic, and culturally liberating potentials.

The solidarity of progressive U.S. Jews with their natural workingclass allies among Arabs, Israelis, and U.S. people of color is the only road to making permanent change that will save everyone on this planet.

Hang in there! Become a prominent Left Jewish spokesperson yourself.

Together in the ghetto: Blacks and Jews in NYC must ally against city establishment

1991

by Emily Woo Yamasaki and Stephen Durham

Racism and anti-Semitism, police brutality, and the rage of the oppressed: these fueled the three-way battle among Blacks, cops and Hasidic Jews in Crown Heights in August 1991.

Anger against decades of institutional racism in New York City caused this conflagration.

But how did the legitimate anger of the Black majority in one of the largest U.S. Black ghettos get channeled into anti-Semitic violence? How do we defeat the divide-and-conquer tactics that pit Jews against Blacks and Blacks against Jews? What do we need to do to go forward together toward a world based on solidarity and mutual respect? How can the Left turn misdirected wrath around and galvanize all the oppressed to fight ignorance, poverty, and genocide?

To know how to advance requires identifying the fundamental problem. This is capitalism, a political and economic system in irreversible decline, careening on the edge of chaos and cynically using ideologies like racism and anti-Semitism to maintain itself by dividing its victims —with explosive results.

The world's first great 20th century city is a time bomb on a short fuse.

Death of Gavin Cato

On a summer afternoon, a driver in the motorcade of the world leader of the Lubavitcher community, headquartered in Brooklyn's Crown Heights, lost control of his car.

The car lurched onto the sidewalk and pinned two Black seven-year-olds, Gavin Cato and his cousin Angela, beneath the vehicle. Neighbors and family, including Gavin's Guyanese-American father, gathered instantly, trying to help; police roughly pushed them away and beat them back.

Almost immediately, a volunteer Hasidic ambulance arrived. Because outrage was building in the growing crowd, police ordered the ambulance driver to leave without the children.

Rumors raced through the Black community that the Jewish ambulance service had abandoned Gavin and Angela. Gavin died that afternoon.

An enraged crowd marched from the accident scene to the police precinct station, demanding the arrest of the driver who hit the children.

Within hours, young Black men retaliated by stabbing a Jewish student from Australia, who died at an under-funded city hospital from inadequate medical attention.

Three nights of violent, pogrom-like confrontations ensued. Black rioters broke windows in Jewish homes and firebombed the Utica Gold Exchange. New York's first Black mayor, David Dinkins, was pelted with bottles. Black demagogue Al Sharpton led a march past Lu- **Capitalism, careening on the edge of chaos, cynically uses racism and anti-Semitism to maintain itself.** bavitcher headquarters under the anti-Semitic slogan "Arrest the Jew." Picket signs proclaimed, "Hitler didn't finish the job."

The melee provided an excuse for heightened police-state repression. Right before Sharpton's march, cops swept more than 150 Black youths off street corners, holding them without charges over the weekend.

Racism fuels Black anger

The nationwide destruction of Black communities like Crown Heights has a definite cause, and it isn't a Jewish conspiracy, as some Black purveyors of anti-Semitism allege.

The proportions of the devastation amount to genocide. Blacks are beset with high unemployment, homelessness, government drug-pushing, organized crime, police abuse, educational cutbacks, and gutting of social, human, and medical services.

The 80,000 Blacks in Crown Heights are largely from the Caribbean and West Indies. As first- and second-generation immigrants squeezed by a contracting economy in an increasingly racist and chauvinist society, they live in unsurpassed conditions of poverty and political disenfranchisement. No wonder they are angry.

Crown Heights Jews: clout, but not control

Crown Heights is also home to 20,000 Lubavitcher Hasidic Jews. In the 1930s, this conservative, anti-assimilationist, religious community left rural Poland because of growing anti-Semitism and immigrated to New York City.

In the '50s, many whites left Crown Heights. The Lubavitchers stayed. In the '60s and '70s, the Black immigrant community arrived.

The insular Lubavitchers became the most organized force in Crown Heights. They participated in corrupt, status-quo urban politics by doing what most special interest groups do in Gotham City: they lobbied the Democratic Party boss machine in an attempt to gain power and influence, with some success.

The fact that they have won some special considerations from the white-dominated city government opens them up to charges of racism, as does their religious philosophy of disdain for the rest of the world—which shows up in everyday life as disdain for the problems of their Black neighbors.

On top of this, Lubavitchers attract resentment because of their support for Israel's right wing, with its policy of constant racist repression of Arabs.

Anti-Semitism mis-identifies the enemy

But with all this said, the Lubavitchers are still merely *players* in the capitalist game—albeit ones holding much better hands than their ghetto neighbors. Anti-Semitism falsely identifies the Lubavitchers—and all Jews—as the *dealers* of the cards.

Scapegoating Jews covers up the role of those who really wield power. This subterfuge operates with historic force. In the transition from feudalism, gentile merchants were the principal force of emerging capitalism. They campaigned against the Jews, who were early traders, using violence, incarceration, and theft of property.

Once entrenched, capitalism nurtured anti-Semitism to deflect the anger of small shopkeepers and small businesses frustrated in their uneven competition with the big bourgeoisie.

Stereotypes like the "international Jewish banking conspiracy" or "Jewish control of the media and Hollywood" are nonsense, although nonsense with a purpose. Far from Jews controlling the system, capitalism in crisis hits Jews with a deadly force—as the Holocaust testifies.

Cultural nationalism fosters bigotry

In the Black movement, the mouthpieces of anti-Semitism are Black nationalists—advocates of an impossible cultural, separatist, and capitalist solution to Black misery. The cultural nationalist program is a volatile mix of anti-Semitism, sexism, heterosexism, anti-Leftism, and anti-workingclass ideology.

The anti-Semitic strain in Black nationalism was clear after Gavin Cato's death. Reverend Sharpton, espousing reactionary Black cultural nationalist politics, preached that Black militancy should be directed against Jews; African American professor Leonard Jeffries charged Jews with being part of a "conspiracy to annihilate Blacks."

The reason the explosion in Crown Heights is so horrifying is that it shows how the anti-Semitism being espoused by political messiahs can strike an answering chord among exploited and hyper-oppressed groups.

The door is then open for fascist organizers to move in and take the lead in violence and murder against Jews.

And after that, who's next?

Radicals must make sure this scenario does not come to pass.

Fight the power together

Leftists can explain how Black-Jewish infighting benefits only the ruling class, allowing it to carry on its dirty work against Blacks, Jews, political radicals, Latinos, Asian and Native Americans, women, lesbians and gays, and all the downtrodden.

To lead, the Left itself must be able to identify and combat anti-Semitism as vigorously as it does racism. Many leftists failed to do this after Crown Heights, out of either unconsciousness of anti-Semitism's importance or unwillingness to criticize Black leaders.

The Left must *act now*. Black and Jewish radicals can rebuild solidarity by spearheading mutual fights against concrete common problems.

The precedent for Jews and Blacks to work as *allies*, not antagonists, is strong. The two groups have a long history of militant and successful collaboration, going back to the founding of the NAACP in the early 1900s. During the civil rights movement, Jewish attorneys risked lives and careers to defend Black clients against the southern police state. At the same time, Black organizers resisted pressure exerted by liberal donors to sever ties with these lawyers because of real or alleged communist affiliations.

This kind of powerful united front is needed again today. The common enemies haven't changed: the neo-Nazis and Ku Klux Klan; a ruling class intent on exploiting and scapegoating both Blacks and Jews.

Shared oppression is the basis today for solidarity between Jews and Blacks. Cementing this solidarity will bring about a new political integration in opposition to the divisions and forced segregation created by capitalism and will, finally, help bring us all closer to a system where no social oppression exists—socialism.

Turning rage into resistance: Solidarity challenges San Francisco cop crackdown

1992

by Merle Woo

I n the late afternoon on May 8, 1992, more than 1,000 people gathered at Mission Dolores Park in San Francisco for a rally and march called by Roots Against War (RAW), a youth of color organization, and other groups. The event was held to support the L.A. rebellion against the acquittal of the cops who beat Rodney King and to protest the massive arrests of demonstrators on the same issue in S.F. on April 30 and May 1.

The cops, who consider that the Simi Valley verdict gives them carte blanche, were ready. Anticipating a slew of new arrests, they had even appropriated a squad of old red and orange Muni buses and painted them black and white, the San Francisco Police Department colors!

When my colleague Moisés Montoya and I arrived at Dolores Park, we could see a line of cops getting into place along the top of the hill, forming a threatening silhouette that blocked the setting sun.

Periodically, SFPD sound trucks blared the message that the rally had to stop and we had to begin our march. The cops' aim was to stop our ideas from getting out by disrupting the rally. We ignored them.

Most of the speakers were angry people of color. They brought out that there have been thousands of Rodney

Kings; democracy and equality are a cruel hoax. Poverty, unemployment, homelessness and racism must go, they said.

A young Black woman from the East Bay Coalition for Justice called for a general strike.

I spoke, saying that we are seeing the start of a class war—not a race war. Together, workers and poor people of all colors are the majority, and we will win against the rich ruling class.

Four other Asian American women, two of them lesbians, declared that they will not be left out of movement leadership, patronized as "model minorities," or used as a wedge by whites against Blacks. The multiracial crowd roared in approval.

And we began to march, chanting *"No justice, no peace!"*

Stripped of our rights, our solidarity grows

One block away from our goal, Duboce Park, a barricade of cops in riot gear forced us to reverse direction. Then a baton-swinging troop rushed the crowd and divided us. Several hundred protesters wound up in a parking lot. The more than 500 who were jammed together on the sidewalk across the street, including Moisés and me, were arrested.

When an impromptu open-mike speak-out developed, about eight cops violently seized the man carrying the sound system and arrested *him.*

We were bound with cutting plastic handcuffs and crammed into buses and vans. My van-mates and I bolstered each other up by singing, "We Shall Not Be Moved," "Solidarity Forever," and "The Internationale."

We were delivered to Pier 38 and dumped into a filthy warehouse there. Five hundred of us shared two telephones, two portable toilets, and two water dispensers.

The group discovered that the cops planned to bring heavier charges against those who had also been arrested the week before. Moisés and I helped lead a discussion in which we collectively decided that we would *all* remain until *all* were released. "Seconds go first!" we chanted.

Eventually, some second-timers were released, which lulled many firsts into leaving, too. Moisés and I and about eight others decided to wait and watch.

The seconds who were held through the night were all out-front activists, including leaders of RAW and ACT UP. They were cited at Pier 38, driven to the Hall of Justice, and then released. The cops wanted to terrorize them by dividing them from the rest of us and messing with them like cats playing with mice.

Most of the demonstrators were accused only of failure to disperse or to obey traffic lights and their charges were dismissed. But some were booked for looting or shutting down a highway, street, or bridge, and their charges were not dropped.

Changing how the scales are weighted

A huge painting at an intersection at San Francisco State University shows a scale of justice with one side completely weighed down by cops and black-robed judges. The students who produced it recognize that there is no righteousness in our social/economic system.

And the fundamental right to protest—our constitutional freedom of speech and assembly—is seriously at risk.

As more and more cops shoot people in the ghettos and barrios, crack demonstrators' heads, and raid homes, cars, and work places with impunity, one has to wonder—is a police state on its way?

Cops go berserk for a reason. They are *used* by the state to protect private property, prop up the status quo, and stifle dissent. If the men with the piles of money are feeling threatened, the men and women in blue will be slipped off the leash. A police state is in place when all of society's important institutions are under the control of the cops and the military.

That day is not imminent in the United States. We have the opportunity *now* to seize the initiative, move onto the offensive, and tip the scales with the mass of those for whom justice is long overdue.

New radical leadership is coming from young people of color, especially the women, and lesbians and gays. In fact, the sexual minority community gets the credit for S.F. Police Chief Richard Hongisto being fired after he threatened martial law following the first post-verdict protests.

The fight is on. Moisés and I are plaintiffs in a class-action suit over the arrests and are organizing for a civilian police review board that is independent, elected, and authoritative. We're also in a defense committee pushing for amnesty for *all* arrestees—no matter what the charges!

As Bay Area activists mobilize against the crackdown, confidence is building that no cop tactics can defeat a community that asserts itself, sticks together over principles, and watches out for its most vulnerable members.

Stop cop terror. Justice now!

American Me:
Anti-gang film pulls no punches, but lacks hope

1992

by Gil Veyna

Whether you like it or not, *American Me* carries a wallop, hitting hard at its intended audience —barrio and ghetto youth. The film is no violence-glorifying *Godfather,* but a no-holds-barred indictment of hard-core gangs as self-destructive for youths of color individually and as genocidal for La Raza as a whole.

Director Edward James Olmos plays Santana, the main character. Olmos, an Oscar nominee for his role in *Stand and Deliver,* feels a passionate responsibility to the Chicano community. He does with *American Me* what the rest of Hollywood refuses to do: de-glamorizes violence. The movie is a form of aversion therapy by which Olmos hopes to repel his audience away from gangs, *clicas.*

No scene better shows that gangs are relentlessly terminal than the death of a young man called Little Puppet at the hands of his own brother. After leaving prison, Little Puppet renounces his affiliation with EME, the "Mexican mafia," an all-powerful *clica* run by Santana. Gang solidarity insists that an example must be made of Little Puppet, and his older brother is blackmailed into killing him. Little Puppet's plans for a future outside of gang life are cut short when his brother slips a rope around his neck and strangles him—all the while demanding in anguish that Little Puppet not look at him.

Meanwhile, Santana has also had a change of heart. Because he refuses to authorize the killing, he is knifed to death by fellow EME members.

Olmos effectively horrifies with one depiction after another of rape, torture, and murder. But if he wants to slam the door on gang life, he needs to open it to something else. This is where the film falls short.

Mujeres with *corazón*, but no hope

What humanity this bleak movie does possess lies in the women. They are the child-rearers, homemakers, communicators, nurturers, cohesive community force, confronters of the corrosive elements of machismo, and yearners after a different tomorrow.

A Chicana single mother, Julie, becomes involved with Santana while he is between prison terms. In a supercharged scene, Julie accuses Santana of betraying La Raza and *el movimiento* by recruiting his people to a life of dead-end brutality. She refuses to accept his excuses and bluster, but she ends her appeal to him by saying, "It's hopeless."

She survives, and her enrolling in school near the movie's end is meant to be positive. But it just seems tangential to all the horror going on around her, and the struggle it takes to *get* an education—especially as a single mother—is not addressed.

There is an imbalance of too much emphasis on the futility of life for young men of color in the barrio without the sense of a world outside being conveyed, and the film's halfhearted message that education is a possible escape route fails to convince.

La lucha left out

American Me is searing and well-intentioned, but also claustrophobic. I wanted it to provide a sense of the movement, of *la lucha,* the struggle, La Raza, the people, something to counter the doom and gloom. Missing was any concrete acknowledgment of the militancy of people of color in the real fight for equality.

I wish the film had asked *why* such deadly *clicas* exist and who benefits. I believe they are the excrement produced by a sick society. Young men of color are capitalism's "waste." With no jobs and no productive role, they are society's rejects. They in turn reject society, becoming parasites on their communities, where their existence is used as a pretext for a police-state presence.

Our self-worth as people of color is undermined by racism and unemployment, and all poor and workingclass youth experience a sense of nihilism about the future. Gangs provide a faulty sense of empowerment which turns frustration and rage inward toward the community and makes cultural pride and maleness synonymous with sexism, homophobia, brutality, and inter-ethnic feuding.

But we know the enemy! I wanted *American Me* to point the finger, to lash out at the institutions and racist cops that try to keep us in check. The only antidote to gangs is vanquishing the system that creates them.

¡La lucha continúa!

We are the leaders we've been waiting for

1993

by Moisés Montoya

U ntil recently, Tom Boot was a prominent Black
comrade in the Freedom Socialist Party and its
San Francisco Bay Area organizer. In October
1991, Boot quit the party with Roanne Hindin and
Constance Scott, two white leaders in both FSP and its
sister organization, Radical Women.

The three were fleeing from the leadership of people
of color, particularly women. More and more, they had
been running a Stalinist-style branch where criticism came
from the top down; Scott, the national RW organizer, and
Hindin, her assistant, were exempt. Members were just
expected to do the work, and our weaknesses rather than
strengths were played up. Because people of color made
up half the branch, this fostered a racist climate.

Scott had enlisted Hindin and Boot, her housemates,
as supporters in a power play with the party's National
Office (N.O.) in Seattle. The three found new ammunition
when two Seattle members were racist toward comrades
of color. They tried to use these incidents to pit the Bay
Area branch against the National Office.

When the Bay Area comrades of color began to
question the trio's motives and demand accountability and
party loyalty from them, the three persuaded a few white
female colleagues that they were being victimized by a Big
Bad Marxist Machine, and then left in a hurry, taking their

clique recruits with them.

Cynical manipulation of race issues

Boot, Scott, and Hindin defected because they couldn't win the Bay Area FSP to their view about how to deal with racism. Their wrong position was that the white members responsible should be witchhunted, persecuted, and driven out of the party.

The Bay Area Comrades of Color Caucus disagreed with this method. Bay Area CCCers wanted to correct the racist mistakes through education and drawing **We people of color who stayed with Bay Area FSP and RW find Trotskyist feminism speaks to our experience.**

the lessons needed to move on. To this end, current Bay Area FSP Organizer Nell Wong and National RW Organizer Nancy Reiko Kato traveled to Seattle to present a resoundingly successful weekend-long race relations seminar for the party and RW.

The BACCC also began calling the trio on their sniping at the FSP National Office. The quitters then labeled us as N.O. dupes and tokens and branded the National Office as kowtowing white liberals (ignoring the comrades of color in leadership). Now that *we* were criticizing *them,* they suddenly accused FSP and RW of being undemocratic.

The discrimination and high-handedness that Boot, Scott, and Hindin charged the N.O. with was really coming from them. They were the ones sabotaging the potential of the comrades of color. They were the aspiring bureaucrats who wanted to run things their way and keep members and the National Office in the dark.

In sum, they no longer agreed with the FSP's revolutionary-integrationist program, support for the leadership of people of color, and democratic methods.

Running from the front lines

According to the party-bashers, Boot's membership in their clique as an African American gay man is supposed to prove that FSP and RW are racist.

Boot dedicated many years to fighting for the leadership of women, people of color, and sexual minorities in the movements. With Chicana FSP leader Yolanda Alaniz, he founded the Seattle Comrades of Color Caucus, which became national.

But the Left, including FSP and RW, is not immune from the pressure of increasing racism in society, as recent splits and strife show. Over time, Boot internalized the stereotypes of minorities as second-class citizens. Like his co-factionalizers, he underestimated the capabilities of other Bay Area comrades of color who were Asian American and Chicano. In other words, Boot, once a staunch fighter for race liberation, turned into his opposite. When we demanded that he reckon with us on his political differences, he took this as a personal affront—and quit.

This schism is not about personalities. It is about *fundamental political disagreements*.

The FSP believes that this profit system has to go. To get rid of it, we need a highly trained organization—a Leninist vanguard party—led by the most oppressed workers, because those who face the most searing abuse are the best fighters.

The deserters no longer believe this.

Boot came to depend on Scott and Hindin socially, politically, and financially. Demoralized, he lost the courage to continue as a leader. Despite his accomplishments, Boot's own sexism, racism, and cultural nationalism—reflected in his posture that, as a Black man, he was above criticism from other members of color—overcame him.

Our time has come

Not coincidentally, most of us who stayed with Bay Area FSP and RW are people of color. We were drawn to

Trotskyist feminist politics because the solution it poses speaks to our experience.

What happened in this internal fire storm validates our program. In this branch, the comrades of color have taken the reins. We're more critical and up-front. What the movements need now is bold and radical leadership from those at the bottom. That's what we intend to continue building. We *are* the leaders we've been waiting for.

For the good of Palestine and Israel: Bring the political exiles home!

1993

by Raya Fidel

On December 17, 1992, the Israeli government dumped more than 400 Palestinians into a barren no-man's-land in southern Lebanon to collectively punish all Palestinians for the death of an Israeli soldier. As a Jew born, raised and educated in Tel Aviv, I condemn the expulsion of the Palestinian deportees.

I have long felt that Israel must return the occupied territories and allow Palestinians to form a state—as the first step in building a joint, socialist state governed by both peoples. But as long as Israel continues to occupy the West Bank and Gaza, it is responsible for the well-being of the inhabitants.

Israeli rationales don't wash

The deportees were primarily highly educated men against whom no charges could be brought because no evidence exists that any of them are linked to the soldier's death. The Islamic organization Hamas took responsibility for the killing, so Israel "justified" its action by claiming that the deportees are Hamas supporters.

Israel was later forced to admit that some of the deportees had been seized by mistake.

The conditions under which these men are trying to

survive remind me of descriptions of the death camps in Bosnia.

On exposed, rocky ground, the Palestinians live in flimsy tents in sub-zero weather. The Israeli government refuses to allow the Red Cross to provide food and medical aid and has even tried to prevent villagers in the area from helping. Some of the men are in serious need of medical care, but only a few have been permitted to receive it.

Despite their cruel actions, Israeli officials deny any responsibility for the fate of the deportees. Instead, they blame the Arab world—particularly Lebanon and Syria— for not taking the men into their countries. Israel has always done this to cover up its racism and ethnocentrism.

This repellent violation of universal ethical and human values makes no sense to me. First, the Jewish tradition is humanistic. Every life is precious both for itself and for the progeny it will bring forth. Jews of the Diaspora fought to end suffering of all people, knowing that oppression against anyone would lead to the suffering of Jews as well.

Second, the deportations achieved the exact opposite of Israel's stated goal. Instead of intimidating the Palestin-

John Bourque/Freedom Socialist

ian community and dissuading it from further protests against occupation, waves of massive demonstrations sweep the occupied territories, another Israeli is killed, and the Palestinian delegation withdraws from the peace talks.

This outcome is hardly surprising: on every Passover, we are reminded that the harder the Egyptians pressed the children of Israel, the stronger became the resistance of our oppressed ancestors.

The Israeli government is obviously ignoring this ancient lesson.

Zionism is the cause of this injustice

Why does the government of the Jewish state ignore the lessons of Jewish history and act in such an un-Jewish manner? Because the government is Zionist.

Zionism is a nationalistic ideology which is based on the assumption that Jews are the only legitimate owners of the "promised land." The ideology is fanned today by memories of the Holocaust and is embellished by U.S. oil interests in the Mideast.

Spurred by intense European anti-Semitism in the 19th century, the growing Zionist movement called on Jews to emigrate to Palestine—blind to the fact that the area was already densely populated.

The Israeli regime perpetuates this blindness, but the Palestinians persistently rebel.

In response, Zionism evolved into a blatantly racist ideology.

The right wing of the Zionist movement makes no effort to disguise its racism. Early on, Menachem Begin declared that the Palestinians were beasts with two legs; former Prime Minister Yitzhak Shamir claims Arabs have no respect for human life and enjoy murder.

As an Israeli child, I was taught in school that the Arabs were not human beings like us, that they didn't need to eat more than a few olives a day, and that they would stab you in the back no matter how friendly they might seem.

This Zionist ideology also governs the justice system. The Israeli Supreme Court declared the deportations to be legal and usually allows Jewish rightwing fundamentalists to go unpunished when they murder innocent Palestinians.

The Palestinian uprisings *(intifadeh)* of the last several years clearly show that faced with continuing oppression, resistance ever intensifies.

And Zionism, born out of the desire for a secure Jewish homeland, will inevitably lead to destruction of that very Home.

End expulsions by ending U.S. aid

We in the U.S. can help prevent the twin disaster to both Palestinian and Jewish peoples without spending a dime for troops. We can do this by halting the billions in U.S. aid for Israeli aggression.

Countless Jews like myself in Israel, America, and around the world call on President Clinton and the new U.S. Congress to cut off all support to Israeli militarism and to return the deportees. Israel's security rests not in missiles but in collaboration with its co-inhabitants and neighbors. Jews will never be safe while Arabs are exterminated.

Hope for the Middle East resides in achieving Arab-Jewish harmony, which in turn must rest on a rejection of imperialist values and the creation of a mutually beneficial socialist sharing of resources, knowledge and common goals. Two great peoples *can* live together—communally.

After Chávez:
Where next for the UFW?
1993

by Yolanda Alaniz

I n an editorial called "César Chávez: The Reality" (*Houston Chronicle,* May 4, 1993), Daniel Suldran wrote: "There are lessons to be learned from the lives of great people. But they are instructive only if we look honestly at how they lived."

Workers and oppressed people owe Chávez a great deal for his unwavering commitment to farmworker organizing. He was a central catalyst in the many trail-blazing victories of the United Farm Workers—winning contracts, initiating effective boycotts, raising wages and improving field conditions. But Chávez also made tragic mistakes. The best tribute we can pay him is an objective assessment of his political legacy that will help advance the movement to which he devoted his life.

Winning ingredients

César Chávez and Dolores Huerta, founders of the association which in 1973 became the United Farm Workers of America, AFL-CIO, led the young union to a string of dynamic accomplishments. As Megan Cornish and I wrote in *The Chicano Struggle: A Racial or A National Movement?*:

> Early UFW successes emerged from an unbeatable combination of factors. The early leadership was

brilliant, audacious and dedicated. It was sensitive to and pushed forward by the masses of insurgent farmworkers. The union gained immeasurably from the instant support provided by the civil rights, Chicano and radical student movements, and by...national labor.

Courageous and winning tactics grew out of this labor/civil rights synthesis. Strikes and boycotts reinforced each other as anti-labor injunctions were openly defied. As a social movement, UFW built a multiracial union, encouraged the involvement of women, and did not exclude...energetic support from the Left.

Chávez retreats from militant action

For the most part, the union's early gains have been lost. Today farmworkers live in worse conditions and earn less than they did 15 years ago. UFW once claimed 100,000 members; today it reportedly has fewer than 10,000 members under contracts. Meanwhile, UFW continues to concentrate on boycotts, now a substitute for strikes rather than an adjunct to them, and neglects union organizing.

What stalled the movement?

• Reliance on Democrat Party politicians, as in 1968 when Chávez pulled seasoned organizers from the fields and assigned them to campaign for Robert Kennedy for president.

• Compromises with labor bureaucrats, for instance the 1974 shutdown of the secondary boycott of Safeway to appease the AFL-CIO brass.

• Obsession with religion, which transformed militant pickets and demonstrations into meek prayer vigils and Masses.

• Unswerving pacifism, which during strikes led to forswearing physical defense in favor of fasting for non-violence.

- Campaigns against "illegal" immigrants, like the 1968 one in which the union reported undocumented workers to the U.S. Border Patrol.
- The development of bureaucratic practices and paranoid anti-communism, which drove out many of the people most dedicated to the union's original aims.

No middle ground

The excruciating '90s demand that UFW rearm itself to represent its constituents. If the union is willing to *learn* from Chávez's life—to emulate his absorption in championing the most exploited workers but abandon the treacherous policies which hold *la causa* back—it can still fulfill its mandate.

What we wrote in *The Chicano Struggle* is even more clearly true today:

> Any effective labor union—particularly one that represents the most exploited workers—must recognize the fundamental and irreconcilable division between the owning class and the laboring class. A union that tries to make peace with the capitalists or their representatives in the Democrat and Republican parties will inevitably be compromised to the point of becoming an intrinsic part of the total system of oppression...
>
> These are the stark options facing the UFW—to be a tool of the bosses or a revolutionary leadership. There is no middle ground... Change [in the UFW] will require convulsive reversals on almost every score:
>
> 1. The union must become *democratic,* with vastly increased local control, rank-and-file decision-making, free speech and the free flow of ideas, and a repudiation of red-baiting.
>
> 2. The union must *break with the Democrat Party* [and] call for a Labor Party.
>
> 3. UFW must *separate itself from the Catholic Church,* the ideologue of pie-in-the-sky and working-

class martyrdom here on earth.

4. It must drop the self-defeating principle of *pacifism* and adopt a policy of organized self-defense against grower violence.

5. The UFW must find its support among militant labor, the movements of the most oppressed, and radicals—those with no stake in the system, who will not try to shroud the movement in accommodationist deals.

6. The union must totally and irrevocably take a principled stand for *the rights of undocumented workers*. It must drop all U.S. chauvinism and prioritize the organization of "illegals"...

If the union adopts these options, it will have within its grasp the opportunity to once again become a dynamic social/labor movement. It will become a radical movement for workers' power because that is the only solution to the enormous weight of oppression suffered by farmworkers.

The impetus for these changes will arise from the farmworkers themselves. They will force the union to meet their needs or get out of the way. As the farmworkers have proven time and time again, when they are ready to move they will explode into action.

And when they do, they will ignite the whole of both the Chicana/o and labor movements. *¡Sí, se puede!*

No "Gold Mountain" for Chinese immigrants

1994

by Emily Woo Yamasaki

My *gung-gung* ("grandfather" in Chinese) arrived at the U.S. immigration port of Angel Island after an inhuman voyage at sea. He was detained on the island for a year and a half.

After diligently preparing himself for the tricky naturalization test, grandfather won citizenship only to end up working two jobs to survive. He supplemented his low wages as a butcher in Chinatown during the day by gambling at night—which meant spending part of his income to pay off the cops.

Since my grandfather made his home here, very little has changed for Chinese immigrants, who have been targets of economic abuse and scapegoating since the mid-1800s. In recent months, the government and media have seized on smuggling incidents like the one involving the Golden Venture, the rusty tramp steamer that ran aground off Queens, New York, in June 1993, to increase anti-Chinese hysteria.

In its cargo hold, the Golden Venture carried nearly 300 people in cramped and unsanitary conditions similar to those my grandfather endured. Some passengers had been aboard for six months. Food and drinking water were scarce. When the ship ran aground, crew members urged the panicked travelers to jump into the cold, pounding surf and swim for shore. Ten died.

The survivors were thrown in jail, thanks to a Clinton policy enacted just weeks before. They will stay there until immigration judges rule on their asylum claims, which may take two years.

A month after the Golden Venture beached, President Clinton introduced legislation to tighten already restrictive entrance policies. His bill would provide for stricter screening of applicants abroad; make it much easier and quicker to reject and deport asylum-seekers; and add 600 officers to the border patrol. In motivating his callous proposal, the president declared, "We will not surrender our borders to those who wish to exploit our history of compassion and justice."

Such shameless demagoguery from the betrayer of the Haitian boat people! What Clinton *didn't* say was that U.S. borders are open only to those whose labor his capitalist class wishes to exploit.

Criminalizing the victims

Federal officials said the Fuk Ching gang, one of a number of international crime syndicates smuggling people into the country, planned to collect as much as $30,000 from each Golden Venture passenger. Once in the U.S., immigrants often end up in sweatshops to work off their debt to these extortionists or "snakeheads."

Media coverage has focused on the criminal role of the gangs—the predators—to stigmatize Chinese immigrants—their prey—as illegal, alien, and sneakily manipulative of an overgenerous system.

By doing this, the media is cooperating with the government and right wing in an inflammatory campaign to blame "foreigners" for unemployment and social and economic crisis. This racist war on "foreigners" extends to everyone whose skin isn't white, without regard to citizenship.

Racism against Asians functions just as other forms of racism and sexism and homophobia do. They all keep workers divided and at each others' throats and justify poverty-level wages, discrimination, and political disenfranchisement.

Asians in the U.S. are portrayed as especially adept at "making it." Vilified as cunning and dangerous on one hand, they are gushed over as the "model minority" on the other. But the reality of life for the majority of Asian Americans and for Asian immigrants, who toil long hours in restaurants and garment factories for less than minimum wage, is light-years away from the fables of academic prodigies and financial magnates highlighted in glossy magazine stories.

Capitalist ship hits shallow shoals

The first Chinese immigrants called California *Gum Sahn*—Gold Mountain. They sought prosperity, but were worked to death as "coolies" (which means "hard labor" in Chinese). They were indispensable to expanding capitalism, which was gathering steam in gold mining and railroad construction.

Today, capitalism is capsizing. More than ever, it needs cheap labor to stay afloat.

One source of this labor is dissidents seeking to leave countries like China and Russia, where Stalinist-style bureaucracy and totalitarianism hijacked socialist revolutions and set the stage for capitalism to falsely advertise itself as the "democratic" alternative. Workers there are now fleeing chaos and clampdowns.

Another labor pool is made up of refugees and immigrants from places where the U.S. ruling class either props up vicious, near-fascist dictatorships, or has bled the country dry economically, or both: Haiti, most of Central America, the Philippines, etc. Workers from nations like these are lured away by the promise of a better life, however faint.

The U.S. establishment hypocritically rails against the influx of new residents, but it is United States policy that is responsible.

Socialism: the path to Gold Mountain

It is time for Asians to shatter the stereotype of us as the model minority by providing bold, radical political leadership.

We should demand that Clinton's administration ensure full rights for all immigrants and undocumented workers and we should challenge every rightwing attempt to cut off health benefits and public education for immigrants or their children.

But the reality is that as long as capitalists are at the helm of state, whether Democrats or Republicans, newcomers will never find friendly shores. Immigration will continue to be a door that swings open and closed according to the economic and political needs of big business.

I believe there is no better homage to my grandfather than fighting for a *socialist* society, one with no need to manufacture disparity between new arrivals and the already settled. Only under socialism can the U.S. become everyone's Gold Mountain.

Invisible women: Sexism in the Black Panther Party
1994

by Debra O'Gara

T he energizing and fundamental role women play in revolutionary organizations came home to me afresh as I read recent memoirs by former Black Panther Party leaders Elaine Brown and David Hilliard.

Brown's *A Taste of Power: A Black Woman's Story* and Hilliard's *This Side of Glory* show us the reasons for the party's spectacular rise—and also its agonizing fall. The books reveal, directly or indirectly, how sexism helped destroy the Panthers.

Hilliard and Brown both recount their experiences growing up Black and oppressed and learning how to survive. For them, as for many others, the Black Panther Party and its visionary Ten Point Program gave direction and potency to their daily fight against racism. They show how the party's internationalist, integrationist, and social- ist politics grabbed the hearts and minds of Blacks and people of all colors radicalized by war, injustice, and broken promises—in the U.S. and globally.

So what happened?

Brought down by disrespecting women

In *This Side of Glory,* Hilliard relives the war waged on the party by the police and FBI—the infiltration, murders, and arrests. With refreshing honesty, he lays bare the destructive internal trends, fed by the government's dirty tricks, that became entrenched practice: the paranoia that turned comrades against each other, the culture of drugs and gangsterism, and founding hero Huey Newton's progressive isolation and one-man rule.

Hilliard has more trouble, however, in discussing sexism. But he says enough for a reader to conclude that poisoned male-female relations must have played an enormous part in disintegrating the party.

In contrast, Brown's *Taste of Power* vividly describes the pervasive and sometimes brutal ill-treatment female Panthers faced—physical abuse, exploitation as sexual prizes and workhorses, and denigration of their abilities.

As early as 1969, Brown realized women "would have to fight for the right to fight for free- **On paper, the Panthers called for gender equality. But "uppity" women leaders were sabotaged and punished.**

dom." By 1975, she concluded that "the value of my life had been obliterated as much by being female as by being Black and poor."

But, like many Black women, Brown believed then that feminism was strictly for well-off whites, and was put off by the predominant radical feminist ideology of the era—that is, the idea that gender concerns are more important than race issues and that men are the enemy, not capitalism.

Brown admits that she did not always speak out against female subordination in the Panthers. Instead, she concentrated on shoring up her own tenuous leadership position, conferred on her unilaterally by Newton. To stay on top while Newton was in prison, she relied on the "normal" macho enforcement techniques.

She reports that she was finally goaded into action

when Regina Davis, who managed the Panthers' highly praised school, ended up in the hospital. "The Brothers" had beaten Davis up and broken her jaw because she reprimanded a male colleague for not carrying out an assignment.

Brown writes that when she told Newton of her anger over the attack, he refused to break solidarity with the men, challenging her to a debate in the Central Committee. Believing the other women would collapse in a direct confrontation over sexism, Brown says, she literally ran away from the fight, leaving the problem of women's role in the Black Panther Party unaddressed and unresolved.

What happened to Regina Davis illustrates perfectly how women's second-class status devastated the party.

As in every other movement, women were the backbone of all the Panthers' administrative and organizational work, particularly the Survival Programs. It was these community projects—childcare, breakfasts, schools, clinics—that won broad support and counteracted the media image of the Panthers as gun-toting thugs. And when given the chance, the women also showed themselves to be keen thinkers, innovative strategists, and moving orators.

On paper, the Panthers called for gender equality. But instead of being recognized, developed, and utilized, their many unacknowledged women leaders were sabotaged, demeaned, and punished for being uppity. The result was a divided, fatally weakened organization.

Learning from history

As the Black Panther chairperson, Brown had more influence than any other woman. Her failure to challenge female invisibility inside the party was a tragedy not just for the Panthers but for the feminist movement, which relies on the pace-setting contributions of radical women of color to remain healthy, united, and effective.

But, over the years since then, other women of color—writers, union and grassroots organizers, lesbian activists—picked up the torch and showed in life and theory how feminism is an organic part of *every* liberation movement.

Brown and Hilliard, and the incredibly significant party they belonged to, could not break free of the sexism of the time. But learning from their struggles will help today's anti-racist revolutionaries, women *and* men, create a new organization that takes up where the Panthers left off.

NAFTA: Tri-country genocide against indigenous people
1994

by Ann Rogers

O n New Year's Day this year, the Mayas of Chiapas, Mexico, rebelled against the North American Free Trade Agreement. Why? Because its "free trade" policies threaten the inherent rights of the indigenous nations of Mexico, the U.S. and Canada to control their lands and destiny.

NAFTA provides multinational corporations with yet one more weapon in their genocidal war against Native Americans—a tool to abrogate treaties, negate sovereignty, and steal resources necessary for Indian survival.

A cannon aimed by big business

NAFTA was constructed by multinationals and passed into law with the blessing of Republican George Bush and the signature of the "liberal" Democrat Bill Clinton.

It can supersede any Native, federal, or local protections that hinder business's freedom to exploit labor, resources, and markets.

One example of how this will work was demonstrated in 1991 under the rules of the General Agreement on Tariffs and Trade (GATT, a global pact similar to NAFTA). U.S. environmentalists had succeeded in getting a law passed to ban tuna imports from countries that killed more than 20,000 dolphins annually during tuna catches. Mexico challenged this law as an "illegal restriction on trade," and an international GATT panel ruled in Mexico's favor.

NAFTA's provisions, designed without input from indigenous peoples, directly conflict with the responsibility the U.S. government has to protect tribal lands and resources.

The legal codes that ensure Native rights to territory and self-governance will be deemed barriers to foreign corporate investment, just as laws protecting labor and the environment will be, so that mega-companies can appropriate Native lands and the minerals they contain. Like GATT, NAFTA sets up an "independent" tribunal that will decide if a law inhibits free trade.

NAFTA allows multinationals to cross borders unhampered. But it does nothing about racist immigration laws that block indigenous people from following these corporations in search of jobs. It has nothing to say about granting free access across dividing lines to people who belong to Native nations split by the borders of the U.S. with Mexico and Canada, such as the Mohawk and the Colville-Okanagan.

"Free trade" expands the international freedom of capital and the slavery of labor.

Legal theft of Native resources and land

In recent years, Native Americans have succeeded in reclaiming many of their treaty rights. For example, in the U.S., the Puyallup tribe won a large claim to tidal areas in Washington State that big businesses had stolen from the Indians decades ago and intensively developed.

NAFTA will make it much harder for indigenous people to win these land claims.

In anticipation of the pact's ratification, former President Salinas of Mexico gutted Article 27 of the country's constitution, abolishing the ancient territorial rights and the *ejidos* (communal lands) of the Mayas. This paved the way for non-Native speculators to grab these valuable properties for large cattle, timber, and farming operations, and it forced many of the peasants who were thrown off their lands into the cities, to become a desperate source of cheap labor.

The Free Trade Agreement between the U.S. and 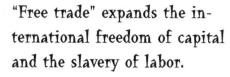 "Free trade" expands the international freedom of capital and the slavery of labor.

Canada, a NAFTA predecessor in effect since 1988, gave the U.S. access to Canadian water and electricity. Now, under NAFTA, Canada cannot reduce the amount of these products it exports to the U.S. unless it reduces its domestic consumption by the same percentage.

To supply multinational aluminum industries in Canada and maintain exports to the U.S., hydroelectric projects involving massive dam systems have been built on Native lands in Canada, destroying Native homelands and hunting and fishing resources.

In Québec, the James Bay project has made the traditional Cree and Inuit ways of life impossible, threatening their survival. In British Columbia, the Kemano project has flooded traditional homelands of the Carrier and Cheslatta nations and reduced the Nechako river to a trickle, devastating the dwindling salmon population.

Organizing to stop the assaults

Indigenous peoples are fighting these free-trade-inspired projects, just as they have fought land theft and treaty sabotage for centuries. Many of the affected tribes are currently organizing international protests of the recent round of betrayals.

NAFTA itself was vehemently denounced by many Native organizations (such as the American Indian Movement and the Continental Commission of Indigenous Nations, Organizations and Peoples) as a clear giveaway of indigenous self-determination by the three North

American governments.

But indigenous people by themselves cannot stop NAFTA, any more than the trade unions or environmentalists can. The separate groups harmed by the North American Free Trade Agreement—Native peoples, labor, and ecologists—must come together across national borders to organize as one. We have common goals that can be realized only in an international united front against our common enemy, international big business.

Radicals of color tackle topics from Native rights to multiracial unity

1995

by Moisés Montoya

J ust two short weeks after the racist, anti-immigrant Proposition 187 was voted in at the California ballot box, a group of activists of color gathered in Oakland for our third national meeting.

The plenum of the National Comrades of Color Caucus (NCCC) of the Freedom Socialist Party and Radical Women, like the ongoing organizing against Proposition 187 happening in the courts and in the streets at the same time, showed that people of color are tough, determined leaders who are not about to let their rights be stripped away and their achievements rolled back.

Team leadership in action

Black, Latino, Asian, and Native members of FSP and RW converged from across the U.S. for the plenum, held November 25-27, 1994. Guests in attendance included one of our Jewish comrades and a special participant from Australia, Bundjalung (Aboriginal) elder Charles Moran.

National Caucus Coordinator Yolanda Alaniz opened the meeting with a keynote address on effective team-building: how to mount a collective effort not to win money or trophies, as more familiar teams do, but in order to make a revolution on U.S. soil.

Other features included an evaluation of our activism in the people of color movements; international reports on the Australian Aboriginal struggle and on embattled Cuba; a discussion of the similarities and differences between the Chicano and Native American movements; an examination of the caucus's impact on the party and RW; and a motivational report on recruitment.

Putting on the plenum gave us all a chance to learn or improve skills, something I especially gained from as one of its organizers. This emphasis on training was continued in skills workshops held on finances, administration, setting priorities, and writing for the press.

A sumptuous Chinese banquet in nearby Berkeley rounded out our rewarding weekend.

Getting the global overview

Charles Moran, the Bundjalung elder from Baryulgil, New South Wales, reported on Aboriginal workers there, who are fighting for redress of injuries brought on by over three decades of mining raw asbestos. Moran showed how Aboriginal struggles in Australia for things like land rights, cultural preservation, and self-determination are similar to Native American battles in the U.S.

Noting that events in one country affect the other, Moran asserted that oppressed people the world over have a common enemy, the globally integrated capitalist system. He concluded that international socialism, a method of organizing society to meet the needs of the many instead of filling the bank accounts of the few, is the only answer.

Chicano labor activist Gil Veyna sounded the same theme in a presentation on the situation in Cuba and FSP and RW organizing in defense of the Cuban revolution.

U.S. businesses hope that the vicious U.S. embargo against the island will lead to the reintroduction of capitalism there. But Fidel Castro and the Cubans have said,

"¡Gracias pero no!" ("Thanks, but no thanks!"), and international opposition to the blockade is on the rise.

Veyna reviewed the highlights of FSP and RW's intensive involvement in anti-embargo work, which has included participation in several of the aid Friendshipments organized by Pastors for Peace. It has also included discussion of what political course the Cuban government needs to steer so that the revolution survives. We are the foremost champions of an internationalist outlook, full workers' democracy, and attention to the needs and ideas of those most affected by the crisis—women, lesbians and gays, and Afro-Cubans.

During the weekend we held our plenum, these perspectives, plus concrete proposals for international support actions, were being raised in Havana by an FSP representative to the first World Conference in Solidarity with Cuba.

Revolutionary integration vs. cultural nationalism

The similarities and differences between Native Americans and Chicanos were reported on in a joint presentation by Debra O'Gara, who is an Alaskan Native, and me, a Chicano—a descendant of Mexicans of mixed indigenous and Spanish heritage.

We identified strong areas of commonality based on our overlapping ethnicity, mutual abuse at the hands of the U.S. ruling class, and shared demands for justice. The main difference we discussed was that Chicanos are not a nation, while Native Americans are. We based this conclusion on Lenin's definition of a nation as an historically evolved, stable community of people, forged on the basis of a common language, territory, economic life, and psychological makeup manifested in a common culture.

For groups who are not nations, identifying as such leads to cultural nationalism: racial/cultural exceptionalism and isolationism coupled with the downplaying of internal class divisions. Cultural nationalism leads to cultural chauvinism, the notion that one's culture is superior to all others.

Agreement with these points by participants was nearly unanimous. Discussion drew out the key point that the media, politicians, and big business are trying to mask *class divisions* in this country by provoking *race war.* It is the job of revolutionaries, especially revolutionaries of color, to show the truths the capitalists are trying to hide and to spearhead multiracial alliances.

Plenty of opportunities to make a difference

In all the movements, FSP and RW members of color have been busy combating the intensified war on workers and the poor and winning people to our socialist feminist politics and organizations. As well as being engaged in all the specific people of color movements, we have had a strong presence in campaigns against the Nazis, against

Rising new leaders of color tour Havana on the 1997 International Feminist Brigade to Cuba: (left to right) Stefani Barber of San Francisco and Cheryl Deptowicz and Bethany Leal of Los Angeles.

U.S. bullying around the globe, and for the rights of immigrants, women, and sexual minorities.

We agreed to increase our efforts in promoting dialogue and solidarity between Blacks and Jews, groups who are pitted against each other both by the ruling establishment and by cultural nationalists. We also agreed to step up our organizing on the job, where all workers of color join together against a common enemy, the boss. Their militancy has ignited the labor movement time and again, and in their hands lies the power to turn this system around.

One of a kind and growing

It was exciting for us to realize that the Comrades of Color Caucus had grown about 30% since our last plenum. The secret to our success is our feminist, Trotskyist program, which speaks to the needs of the most disenfranchised and is the basis on which we have built this unique multiracial and multi-issue caucus. We not only represent the diversity in FSP and RW, but make policy that politically orients our organizations in the people of color movements.

The caucus exists because we believe that the leadership of people of color is vitally needed today. The working class is looking for humane solutions to the overwhelming problems it faces, and the people who currently run our lives have proven that they don't have any. The answers are going to have to come from the bottom up.

International solidarity, support for indigenous struggles, and defense of civil rights, affirmative action, and immigrant rights are at the top of our caucus agenda. We're serious, we're proud, and we've done our homework. It's forward from here—look for us!

California Prop. 187 rings with echoes of Japanese American concentration camps

1995

by Diane Fujino

As I joined in organizing against California's Proposition 187 last year, I flashed back to what happened to my parents and grandparents during World War II. Along with 120,000 other Japanese Americans, mostly U.S. citizens, my family was imprisoned in a concentration camp. The groundwork for this outright violation of their constitutional rights had been laid by a long string of discriminatory statutes.

The government used "national security" as an excuse. Yet, it knew from its own investigations that U.S. Japanese were not a security threat.

How do contemporary assaults on immigrants remind me of this earlier racist treatment of Japanese? Let me count the ways.

Same old scapegoating

Then and now, immigrants are convenient targets to blame for economic problems.

The revolving door of immigration operates according to fluctuating business needs. When the economy is strong, the door cycles in vast numbers of desperate immigrants. But when the economy turns down or the new arrivals resist their super-exploitation, the door expels them.

But never completely, because the profit system is addicted to low-paid immigrant labor. The purpose of periodic immigrant-bashing is not to deport every undocumented worker, but to terrorize newcomers into paralysis and seduce other workers into believing that wage cuts, joblessness, and slashed social services are the fault of dark-skinned "foreigners."

Racism, embedded in this country's origins, will be an integral component of scapegoating as long as capitalism stands.

Popular seal of approval

The bosses' abuse of vulnerable groups succeeds best when legitimized and institutionalized *by other workers*. The ballot box is a handy tool.

The very first initiative in California, Proposition 1, closed loopholes in an earlier law designed to prevent Japanese from buying or leasing agricultural land. Also called the Alien Land Law of 1920, the measure was ratified by voters three to one.

Japanese were recruited to the state as seasonal laborers by agribusiness. They entered an already strongly racist climate; white workers saw immigrants as competition and blamed them for depreciating wages and conditions.

Racism was encouraged not only by openly white-supremacist politicians and media, but by the reactionary leadership of the American Federation of Labor as well. And the AFL had a stranglehold on the state union movement, due to the government and vigilante terrorism that crushed more enlightened labor tendencies as they developed.

But the passage of laws against Japanese farmers only began when they started to make headway as small owners, often by skillfully reclaiming wasteland. Agribusiness saw this as a threat, and so did other family farmers. The new factory farm system spelled the end for small farmers, but they, like white workers, blamed immigrants.

Seventy-five years and 186 propositions later, the ballot box is once again the vehicle for misdirected fury against immigrants.

Twin-party partners in crime

Senator James Phelan, a Democrat struggling for reelection against a projected Republican landslide, sparked Proposition 1. After the Pearl Harbor bombing two decades later, Republican Earl Warren, then the California Attorney General, was a ferocious proponent of Japanese incarceration. In February 1942, Democrat President Franklin D. Roosevelt endorsed Warren's bigotry by signing the order under which Japanese were imprisoned.

Today, only the names have changed. Republican California Governor Pete Wilson tries to revive his career by blaming undocumented workers for the state's financial crisis and championing Proposition 187. Democrat President Bill Clinton wants to increase border-patrol spending by $173 million, tighten the asylum process, and introduce an identification card for all workers.

So much for the "lesser of two evils" in politics.

Power to the people!

However, the past and present are not identical. For Japanese early in the century, life was one repressive statute after another, culminating in internment. But now, even though Proposition 187 passed by a large margin, activists have won court injunctions that, so far, prevent its implementation. Why the difference?

It certainly is not that earlier generations of Japanese didn't fight back. They did, although the information is hidden. They got arrested to challenge the constitutionality of evacuation orders, formed the Heart Mountain Fair Play Committee to resist going to war for the government

Students from the Porterville, California high school and middle school participate in a statewide election day walkout against Proposition 187.

that imprisoned them, and planned demonstrations and organized strikes inside the camps.

But Japanese then did not have the support that immigrants do currently. In 1942, the only organized groups to oppose the wholesale uprooting of Japanese were the Socialist Workers Party, Socialist Party, and Quakers. Today, students, leftists, unionists, feminists, gay activists, and people of all colors are battling Proposition 187. The Black, Chicano/a, and other liberation movements of the 1960s dramatically changed our consciousness, so that we now recognize our collective strength.

Nowhere is the potential for collective strength greater than in the labor movement, and organized labor is learning from its racist past. In the early 1900s, the AFL was the leading advocate for Japanese exclusion. But in the '90s, labor is an entirely different entity due to the influx of women and people of color into the workplace, the internationalization of the work force, and persistent struggles by workers of color to force unions to open their ranks.

As a result, unions now help spearhead the defense of immigrants. Rank-and-file members are cooperating on labor issues back and forth across the U.S.-Mexico border.

Despite all the effort that has gone into keeping people of diverse colors and national backgrounds divided, an uncensored look at all the movements shows that multiracial solidarity crops up again and again, because it succeeds. For example, in 1903 Japanese and Mexicano migrant laborers joined forces against the mighty sugar-beet industry in Oxnard, California—and won.

I've learned important lessons from drawing parallels between the attacks on my family 50 years ago and on immigrants today. We must always fight back for liberation and justice everywhere. And by recovering our history and unifying, we have the power to conquer our common enemies.

What road for healing the divisions between African Americans and Jews?

1995

by *Phillis Whitmore and Adrienne Weller*

Reading *Jews and Blacks: Let the Healing Begin,* by Cornel West and Michael Lerner, an old saying came to mind—if two Jews are in a room talking, you end up with four opinions. Black scholar Cornel West and Jewish writer Michael Lerner certainly have plenty of opinions, most of them inconclusive and self-contradictory.

Their book is obviously well-intentioned and often fascinating. We read it hopefully. As political comrades, one Black, one Jewish, we hoped to find an examination of the conflicts between Jews and Blacks and proposals for concrete steps to resolve them. But what we found were two professional pessimists who dialogued for 276 pages without ever quite saying what the basis is for anti-Semitism among Blacks and racism among Jews.

Liberal non-critique of capitalism

Lerner and West attribute the tensions between Jews and Blacks to a rampant "ethos of selfishness" that can be countered by religious renewal, or nationalism based on spiritual ideals, or an emphasis on personal relations. They offer solutions that are lighter than air to material problems firmly rooted in a specific type of economic system, one that depends on scarcity of opportunity and competition among workers to keep wages down and profits up.

Lerner champions a broad ideology he calls the Politics of Meaning, a philosophy so abstract, non-threatening, all-purpose, and multi-class that even Hillary and Bill Clinton can embrace it.

He thinks that "for Jews...the central question is the nature of Jewish identity." One way for Jews to "get a sense of their value," he says, is "by really reclaiming their religious heritage." He believes that the other route is "through a nation state," the legitimacy of which would be determined by "the extent to which it lives according to God's will"!

Similarly, West sees hope for Blacks in "Christianity's universalistic ethic."

West and Lerner are trying to analyze Black/Jewish antagonism without asking the crucial question: who benefits?

Falling prey to cultural nationalism

Missing the fundamental reason why Blacks and Jews are divided means missing the vital connection they share: the common experience of being exploited, oppressed, and scapegoated by the same enemy.

This makes West and Lerner susceptible to the defeatist mentality that feeds cultural nationalism. West, for example, admits that he thinks "it's unlikely that we'll ever overcome racism."

By cultural nationalism we mean cultural chauvinism and nationalist sentiment among people who don't actually make up a nation, which we define as a community bound together over time by a mutual language, culture, economy, and territory.

Blacks in the U.S. are not a nation—which does not make their freedom struggle any less crucial!

And Jews in Israel are not a historically developed

nation, but an illegitimate settler-state—which does not diminish by an iota the horror of the Holocaust and the need to end anti-Semitism! Jewish nationalism in the U.S. also takes the form of anti-assimilationism, of urging Jews to separate from the rest of society.

West and Lerner do not attempt to spell out exactly what a nation is, and both are ambivalent about nationalism. They believe nationalism is limiting, but find excuses for the nationalism of their own groups.

When Lerner labels anti-Semitic Black nationalist Louis Farrakhan a "racist dog," West defends Farrakhan. West would rather call Farrakhan "a xenophobic spokesperson when...dealing with Jewish humanity." West sees the nationalist aspirations of Blacks as a dead end; but, he says, "The progressive Black nationalist position is the closest I come to."

On the question of Jewish nationalism, Lerner, too, is inconsistent.

On one hand, he criticizes Israel's abuse of the Palestinians and contends that ultimate salvation for Jews "will involve the disappearance of nation states and the creation of an international order."

But until that time, he says, he will "support Jewish national aspirations to protect us from xenophobic nationalism and fundamentalism that still 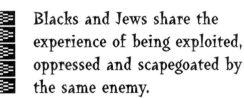 **Blacks and Jews share the experience of being exploited, oppressed and scapegoated by the same enemy.** threaten to use the Jews as the 'demeaned other.'"

He says that to support Zionism—the ideology that robbed Palestinians of *their* homeland—"is simply to support affirmative action on the international scale."

The authors fail to see that the nationalism of both Zionism and the Nation of Islam is as dangerous *to their own communities* as it is to others. This is because reactionary nationalism makes enemies out of people who should be allies and keeps oppressed people hostile to each other and segregated.

Just do it!

West and Lerner are a big disappointment. They flirt with Marxism and tip their hat to feminism, but never commit to a genuine relationship with revolutionary politics, as they must do if they really want to bring Jews and Blacks together.

Tellingly, in West's long (but admittedly incomplete) list of "towering Black and Jewish figures," he leaves out the most incendiary firebrands, like Malcolm X and Karl Marx. For his part, Lerner specifically *rejects* down-to-earth, in-the-streets organizing around concrete daily issues, the only real way to rebuild the sturdy bridge between Jews and Blacks that existed in the civil rights movement of the '60s.

But heroes like Malcolm and Marx are just the models we need. And through united struggle, the healing can begin.

Multiracial strikers persevere against Diamond Walnut

1996

by Imogen Fua

It was October 1995 when I visited the picket lines at Diamond Walnut, peak season for this huge processing plant in Stockton, California. Trucks trickled in and out of its half-empty parking lot.

Five hundred workers with Teamsters Local 601 struck the company in 1991 for employer-paid health benefits and a decent wage. An accompanying boycott has left Diamond with a dwindling pool of customers, forcing it to cut prices this year in an effort to unload stock accumulated in 1993 and 1994.

The strikers are mostly women—Chicanas and Mexicanas, Blacks, whites, and newcomers from southern Asia. Their walkout shows vividly how women and people of color are shaking up traditionally conservative unions like the Teamsters.

Workers such as those at Diamond Walnut almost have no choice but to be militant. In California, especially, they are in the eye of a political storm created by anti-immigrant Proposition 187, a statewide blitz against affirmative action, and the intense regional impact of NAFTA, which encourages runaway shops and the brutal exploitation of undocumented workers.

The Diamond strikers are showing their sisters and brothers in the labor movement how to challenge the corporate tactics of foreigner-bashing and racism and sexism so workers can pull together to win concrete gains in pay and conditions.

Bosses shed crocodile tears

Before the strike, Diamond had been going through difficult times, and management threatened to transfer the factory to Mexico to lower labor costs. Workers pitched in and agreed to a 30% wage cut; Diamond promised to compensate them when it got back on its feet.

By 1991, Diamond was on the Fortune 500 list of most profitable enterprises. But rather than giving its employees back pay, it demanded more concessions.

The workers felt betrayed. Women I spoke with talked about how they regularly went beyond the call of duty to maintain quality work even after wages were cut. Their sacrifices failed to make the company more beneficent.

Frances Evans, a single mom and 10-year employee, told me: "We got a raise of a dime and then had to pay $30 a month for health care insurance, so really we were not getting a raise; they were taking more away from us."

The company has been just as unscrupulous in trying to break the strike and bust the union. It is attempting to get Teamsters Local 601 decertified as the representative of the strikers and current workers. Elections in 1992 and 1993 resulted in the rejection of the union, but both times the union found evidence of management violating labor laws. The National Labor Relations Board is planning a new election.

Battling the corporate Scrooges

Outside the factory gates, I asked retiree Arlene Cutburth what has sustained the long commitment to the strike. "They thought that we old ladies would go away," she said, "but most of us are angry enough to see this through."

Women I spoke with were critical of corporate greed in general, drawing parallels between Diamond and other businesses, like nearby farms that pay their workers the lowest wage legally allowed while their profits skyrocket.

The Diamond strikers are mostly single mothers and women in their 40s and 50s. Many now support themselves in just these kinds of minimum-wage, seasonal, and part-time jobs lacking health benefits. "How do these corporations think we can pay rent, utilities, and medical bills and take care of our children at $4.25 an hour?" asked striker Donna Rickets-Umbel, who is holding down a minimum-wage job full-time.

Many of the strikers fit in time for the picket line on the way home from these low-paying replacement jobs. These rank-and-filers are the backbone not only of the walkout, but of the boycott as well, which they seek support for in visits to stores throughout the area. Strikers have also undertaken a national bus tour, lobbied Congress, conducted a 40-day fast, and traveled to Europe.

The wave of labor's future

As immigrant farmworkers in Stockton, my Filipino grandparents struggled alongside Chicanos/as and other Asian Americans for better treatment—but they were always ostracized by the unions, crippling their efforts against the bosses.

Now women and people of color are the majority of the work force, and they are demanding that unions represent them and stand up for their issues. Women of color especially are taking political initiative and assertively placing themselves center stage. More, they are providing a visionary agenda for the labor movement, one of fighting for an equal sharing of the wealth produced by workers.

By their militance and unity, the Diamond Walnut strikers are helping to point labor in this new direction. As Frances Evans put it, "This is a strike against all corporations and the victory is for all workers."

Looting by multinationals forces Canadian Natives onto warpath over land and resources

1996

by Ann Rogers

While Canada supplies troops for what it falsely calls peacekeeping and humanitarian missions around the globe, it hopes that nobody is watching what its military is doing at the same time at home: namely, committing genocide against Native peoples.

The traditional hunting and fishing grounds of First Nations contain most of Canada's remaining natural resources—water, timber, oil, uranium, and other minerals. More aggressively than ever, the government is cooperating with transnational corporations to steal these resources.

The looting is spurred on by the North American Free Trade Agreement, which can supersede any Native, federal, or provincial law deemed to put up barriers against foreign investment. Basically, NAFTA dictates that what the multinationals want, Canada must provide.

While the corporations reap the profits that result from unchecked exploitation, the First Nations reap pollution of their environment, loss of means of livelihood, illness, and death. In northern Alberta, for instance, drilling and development by Unocal Oil Co. is causing severe health problems and fatalities among the Lubicon

Cree, especially the children.

But the new level of thievery has provoked a new level of defense. Last year, Natives all across the country put their lives on the line to defend their territory. Three examples from a summer and autumn of militancy:

• *Shuswap nation:* This band's fight is over traditional ceremonial grounds at Gustafsen Lake in British Columbia. Though they never signed away this land to Canada, the government granted title to a U.S. cattle rancher.

When Shuswaps tried to reestablish themselves in the area, the government backed up the rancher's claim with the largest mobilization of the Royal Canadian Mounted Police (RCMP) in the country's history—400 troops with heavy artillery and tanks.

After several confrontations, in which one Native was gravely wounded and police claim that two cops were shot but not seriously injured, the RCMP in September surrounded the Natives and arrested them.

Two Gustafsen Lake defenders remain in jail facing attempted murder charges. They are seeking a jury trial in which they can present their case for sovereignty to the public.

• *Kettle and Stony Point nation (Chippewa):* These bands successfully reclaimed the Ipperwash military base in Ontario, which was created on land expropriated from

the Chippewas in 1942 under the War Measures Act. They then occupied nearby Ipperwash Provincial Park, an ancestral burial site.

On September 6, the Ontario Provincial Police moved in and fired on the unarmed Natives, killing Anthony (Dudley) George. In just two days, 2,000 Aboriginal people assembled for George's funeral.

Officials have now acknowledged the Native claim to the Ipperwash territory, although it is not yet certain that they will actually honor it.

• *Nuxalk and Heiltsuk nations:* The B.C. Ministry of Forests gave permission this summer to several logging companies to start clear-cutting the old-growth Great Coastal Forest. But this forest is the traditional home of the Nuxalk and Heiltsuk nations, who have never ceded the land to Canada. In September, after International Forest Products began to blast roads through the forest, the Nuxalk and Heiltsuk blockaded access to King Island.

After an inspiring three-week standoff, the RCMP again attacked, arresting 22 people. The defendants were scheduled for trial and released, some of them after spending three weeks in jail. Refusing to recognize Canada's jurisdiction over them, they are now in hiding.

Youth and women show leadership

Many of the Natives involved in these occupations are young people. They are impatient with the government's endless stalling over land claims and angry about the often desperate quality of life for Aboriginal people, who experience Canada's highest rates of poverty, infant mortality, unemployment, crime, alcoholism, and suicide. It is clear to them that bold action must be taken to halt the steady extermination of their culture and ways of subsisting.

The occupations and blockades are pressuring tribal leaders to be more aggressive, prompting the formation of support groups across Canada, and generally helping to spark a resurgence of Native protest and education in the streets, the courts, and other forums.

In September, for example, Mohawk nation demonstrators in Québec, mostly youth, marched and blocked highways to oppose police assaults against Natives taking back their lands.

Native women are also prominent in the new assertive wave. Shuswap clan mothers, most of whom had sons and daughters embroiled in the Gustafsen Lake face-off, were prepared to meet government force with force.

Youth, women, and many elders know that the survival of their people is tied to retaining sovereignty over their territory. They believe they are responsible for preserving the health of the earth for future generations, and they intend to stop the corporate exploitation that leaves in its wake a polluted wasteland that will last for centuries.

And they are ready to use any means necessary.

Rudy Acuña: Against the odds
1996

Interview by Yolanda Alaniz

R odolfo Acuña is an activist, teacher, historian, and author, most recently of ANYTHING BUT MEXICAN: CHICANOS IN CONTEMPORARY LOS ANGELES. He is also a founder and leading light of Chicano Studies.

Acuña applied in 1990 for a position in the Chicano Studies Department of the University of California, Santa Barbara. Despite his impressive credentials, he was turned down. Members of the department, who had voted to hire him, were overruled by a review committee whose membership UCSB kept secret.

The panel found Acuña's "fiery brand of advocacy" inappropriate and his pioneering scholarship "weak."

Acuña sued the University of California Regents in 1992. On October 30, 1995, he won a milestone victory when a multiracial jury in Los Angeles agreed that he had been discriminated against.

In December, however, Judge Audrey Collins refused to compel UCSB to appoint Acuña to the position in dispute. Instead, she granted him a $325,000 award. Acuña continues to fight for the job he was unfairly denied.

Alaniz: What are the main issues of your case and what is its current status?

Acuña: When we brought the case originally, it was for political, race, and age discrimination. However, the political causes of actions were thrown out on technicalities, and the federal judge, Judge Collins, threw out the race discrimination [charge]. But we went down to the wire on what we had.

We realized that Capital can always whittle you down; they have resources and can pick at you on technicalities. I saw numerous lawyers who did not want to take up the case—not because we did not have a good case, but they thought it would cost too much money. You can not let them get away with this.

We won our verdict. We had a workingclass jury and they found in our favor. UC spent four million dollars and their attorneys were much more seasoned, but we proved they could be beaten.

However, to get the remedy is another thing. UC has been spending an enormous amount of money trying to take attorneys' fees away from my attorneys, trying to take whatever victory we have.

And the judge has denied me reinstatement, saying I created a "hostile environment" because I called UC Santa Barbara a racist institution. She is denying me my free speech rights. According to her logic, they could not have integrated the schools in the South, because Martin Luther King was creating a "hostile environment."

We are probably going to appeal [the judge's decision] on First Amendment grounds. However, we are running out of resources.

It would be easy to take the $325,000. But my feeling is that you cannot take money [for yourself]; it sets a bad example. If we are forced to take money instead of the job, we will start a foundation and use their money to sue them again.

Alaniz: What is the political importance of your case?
Acuña: The main function of a so-called intellectual, because that person has an awful lot of luxury to think and write and do things that other people cannot do, is to

cultivate skepticism. Because without skepticism, you will not have any change, because you will not have any questions.

The American university has been so mystified that people believe it is honestly objective and that it strives for the truth. [But] the knowledge that we gain [from my] case shows that the university serves the superstructure because it creates ideas that support it.

The political importance of the case is that UC had to show us their secret documents. We found out how the university did things. We exposed any illusion of objectivity. For example, UCSB tried to appoint Otis Graham as the chair of the secret ad hoc committee. He is a founder of the Federation for American Immigration Reform [a rightwing anti-immigrant group]. UCSB put Wallace Chafe, a former member of the CIA, on the committee. The most gullible person would ask why.

I was punished for political reasons; if they could have beat me down or beat me in court, I think it would have silenced most Chicano academics.

Alaniz: What kind of tactics did UC use?

Acuña: They launched a campaign to assassinate my character. They made me take a mental examination. They asked me about my political work and sexual preference. They got an order to photocopy my notes. They harassed my wife. They called Chicano scholars throughout the country asking them to testify against me.

We responded by fighting tooth and nail.

Alaniz: What advice do you have for others who face this kind of discrimination?

Acuña: Take them on! Talk to me and my lawyers. Develop a plan.

You have to take it on as a political case. If you don't, you are deluding yourself. The law is made to protect the rich, not the people.

If you win, that is the icing on the cake. Any materials that you develop, put into archives so other people can use them.

Alaniz: What are the challenges facing Chicanas and Chicanos on campuses?

Acuña: The biggest is the faculty government process. It sounds very democratic that the faculty govern the universities. But these same people make the choices of who will attend universities, [by making choices about matters such as] whether to support tuition hikes—which they usually do because their salary goes up.

Latinos will be 67% of the population of Los Angeles in the year 2050. But of the people who are being trained right now in the UC doctorate program, less than 1% are Chicanos. So by 2050, when we will be probably 50% of university students, we will only make up 5% of the faculty.

Alaniz: What is the future for Chicano Studies?

Acuña: It is going to be a hard road. There are no real Chicano Studies programs right now; the only full-fledged department is at Northridge [California State University]. Chicano Studies always depended more on barrio kids— the first generation to attend college. It will be more difficult to meet this goal in the future.

We need to get into the barrio and tell our youth that it is their right to get a higher education.

Alaniz: So how do we organize to meet this challenge?

Acuña: We have to create skepticism. A questioning of truths. We have to confront this system. Marx said that polemics was the engine of struggle. And struggle is the most important part of history.

Asian Americans defy "model minority" myth

1996

by Nancy Reiko Kato

When a reactionary like *Newt Gingrich* expresses concern that affirmative action may be discriminatory against Asian Americans, I have to suspect that we are being set up.

Affirmative action is no longer necessary, according to politicians and their funders; Asian Americans, they tell us, are the example of how old-fashioned hard work and values still open the door to success in the USA.

Hold it—sound the alarms! The reality of racist oppression against Asian Pacific Americans is once again being rewritten into its opposite: the myth of the model minority.

Racist "love" masks exploitation

Our typecasting as the "good" minority is designed to help keep workers of all colors squabbling among ourselves for the approval of the bosses. The ruling class wants us to conform to the stereotype of passive, submissive house boys and geisha girls, devoted to serving their needs and interests.

To accomplish this, they build up the false image of the model minority. Through diligent effort and loyalty to the master, goes their lie, Asian Americans can attain equality without disturbing the status quo. We are held up to other people of color to show how ambition and thriftiness are all that's required to live the American dream.

This is particularly true of the many tenacious small-business owners. But what isn't recognized is that large numbers of Asian Americans come from peasant cultures, where owning a family business, no matter how tiny, is how success is judged. Furthermore, given language barriers on top of racism, these little enterprises that exploit the entire family are often the only avenue of survival open to us once here.

And then our much-exaggerated success is used against us. Portrayed as the Asian menace stealing jobs from "real Americans," we are scapegoated for economic crisis.

Some movement misleaders rise to the capitalist bait, fueling tensions between us and darker-skinned minorities. Louis Farrakhan of the Nation of Islam, for example, labels us "bloodsuckers" because 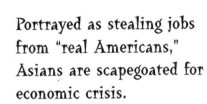 of the Asian American shops operating in Black neighborhoods.

And while the model minority mystique encourages whites to love us for our reputed docility, it also teaches them to fear us, because we may supposedly cost them a job or a school placement.

But if we've made it, why haven't our college degrees resulted in employment opportunities and pay scales comparable to our white counterparts? With so many of us attending college, why are Asian Americans only 1% of college administrators?

Why do Filipino and Korean and Chinese garment workers suffer some of the most torturous labor conditions? Why are 85% of the Cambodians and Laotians in

California's Alameda County, where I grew up, poor?

No, our yellow skin hasn't shielded us from racism. The pattern of discrimination is clear—from early exclusion laws against Chinese and Filipino women that kept Asians and Pacific Islanders from forming stable communities, to imprisonment of Japanese Americans in camps during World War II, up through the current dramatic increase in anti-Asian crimes of violence.

Buying the hype

For the bosses, one of the greatest benefits of the model-minority myth is that it plays up racial divisions among working people. And they are aided, of course, when Asian Americans accept negative depictions of ourselves and other people of color.

This happens in part because our past is hidden. Many Asian Pacific immigrants arrive here already weighted down by stereotypes of other races, but minus the knowledge of vibrant multiracial coalitions that their forebears participated in to win civil rights for all.

But ignorance is not the only problem. Some Asian Americans have a material stake in embracing the pretense of our favored status. When the federal Glass Ceiling Commission interviewed 14 Asian American male executives, not one deemed himself a minority!

In their attempt to secure a piece of the American pie, Asian Uncle Toms will often prove their loyalty to the system by lashing out against people of color. University of California regent Stephen Nakashima, for example, voted to repeal affirmative action at UC.

Refuse to be used by the bosses!

But these sellouts are exceptions, not the rule. Asian American history is bursting with courage, compassion, and collaboration with other oppressed people.

Filipinos joined with their Chicano and Mexicano sisters and brothers to found the United Farm Workers

Union. Asian American students helped lead the Third World strikes at San Francisco State that established Ethnic Studies. Japanese Americans spoke out against the proposal to intern Arab Americans during the Persian Gulf War. Asian American seamstresses have fought for safer conditions and higher pay for all garment-industry workers.

Today, we persist in resistance—especially in the battle for affirmative action, where groups like UC Santa Barbara's Asian Sisters for Ideas in Action Now! (ASIAN!) have come to the fore.

Affirmative action, which Asian Americans were active in winning, has integrated higher education and the work force. It has led to the creation of Ethnic Studies and contributed to breaking down the barriers of racial and sexual bigotry on the job, as women and men of every shade learn together how management exploits them all.

It's no wonder, then, that the right wing has decided it's time to dismantle affirmative action, and is trying to use the model-minority myth to recruit Asian Pacific Americans to this task.

But we won't be their flunkies! Our responsibility is to raise our voices even higher in the fight for justice for our race and our class—the working class. And that is exactly what we will do.

You were born

1997

by Nellie Wong

You were born, sweet child,
from sweat and tears
from blood that flowed
through our veins

You came out of disability
out of skin and teeth
and bones and rage
at inequities
of race, gender, class

You walked out into the sun
with the ferociousness
of a tiger
You teethed in Selma, Little Rock,
in the Third World Strikes
out of free speech
and Blacks who refused
to sit any longer
at the back of the bus

You came in different sizes and shapes,
heights, skin tones
You were hanged, gunned down,
chased out of town, murdered,
sold, put on the auction block

But your humanity shone through
the voices of the Fannie Lou Hamers,
Robert Williamses, Ella Bakers,
and countless unknowns,
the Browns, Yellows, Reds, and Whites
who fought alongside you
who saw a vision of this life,
on earth, on the plains, valleys,
through rivers and forests
and urban sprawls

You were not born
with a silver spoon in your mouth
You came, encumbered with years
of slavery, exploitation
in classrooms, offices,
locker rooms, construction sites

You will walk upright,
across this America
this land where opportunities
are supposed to be available
You will not die
We won't let you
we, with pens in our hands,
we, with energy in our whole bodies,
we, who fought for you and with you,
No, you will not die
You will live and see
that freedom rings
for you are our blood, our passion,
Affirmative Action,
that flows through the maps
of our bodies, of our desire
that vibrates for that epitome,
that coveted prize: freedom

❈❈ CONTRIBUTORS ❈❈

Yolanda Alaniz won 17.5% of the vote in 1991 as the first Chicana to run for Seattle City Council. She coauthored *The Chicano Struggle: A Racial or a National Movement?* and is now a political organizer in Los Angeles.

Tom Boot, for many years a leading Black analyst and activist in FSP, left the Trotskyist movement after a split in the San Francisco Bay Area branch. (See pages 11-12 and 101-104.)

Stephen Durham is a longtime gay militant, hotel and restaurant worker, and FSP organizer in New York City.

Dr. Raya Fidel, a Jewish native of Israel, is an outspoken opponent of Zionism and a professor of library and information science at the University of Washington.

Imogen Fua, a Bay Area feminist, comes from a long line of Filipino American labor activists.

Dr. Diane Fujino teaches Asian American Studies at the University of California, Santa Barbara and is a founder of the campus organization ASIAN! (Asian Sisters for Ideas in Action Now!), which has taken a lead in defending affirmative action.

Cora Harris, an African American feminist, works as a secretary in Brooklyn, New York.

Pat Hirose is a legal secretary in the Bay Area.

Nancy Reiko Kato, National Organizer for Radical Women, is a defender of abortion rights and editor of a law journal at University of California at Berkeley.

Moisés Montoya coordinates the Bay Area Comrades of Color Caucus. He is a Chicano gay leader and an architectural assistant at the City of Oakland.

Henry Noble, a radical Jewish labor organizer in Seattle, is National Secretary of the FSP.

Debra O'Gara works on cases defending treaty fishing and hunting rights as a tribal attorney for the Puyallup Indians in Washington State. She is an Alaskan Native.

Darryl Powell is an African American firefighter in New York City.

Ann Rogers keeps neo-Nazis at bay in the Pacific Northwest through her work in United Front Against Fascism. She is a socialist of Chippewa ancestry.

Gil Veyna, a Chicano hospital worker, is a bibliophile, film aficionado, and Cuba activist in Seattle. He represents his federal employee union on the King County Labor Council.

Adrienne Weller is a Jewish feminist, staunch unionist, and organizer of Portland FSP.

Phillis Whitmore, a talented musician and singer, is an African American campaigner for immigrant and gay rights and against police brutality in Portland, Oregon.

Nellie Wong is an acclaimed poet of Chinese descent. Her writings have been recognized in two permanent plaques installed at public sites in San Francisco. Her books are *Dreams in Harrison Railroad Park, The Death of Long Steam Lady,* and *Stolen Moments.*

Merle Woo won two renowned cases against the University of California for discrimination based on race, sex, sexuality and politics. She is a lesbian Korean-Chinese American poet and author of *Yellow Woman Speaks.*

Emily Woo Yamasaki, an actor, lesbian activist, and office worker in New York City, was one of three feminists chosen to represent Radical Women on a recent delegation to Cuba.

※※※※※ INDEX ※※※※※